ZIPP

The Impact of Henry Hardin Newman

Frances "Bee" Newman Morris

with

Worth Earlwood Norman Jr

© Copyright 2019 Frances Newman Morris

ISBN 978-1949422-931

ARCHDEACON BOOKS

Hoover, Alabama

Contents

Foreword

This book tells the unique story of sportswriter Henry Hardin "Zipp" Newman as revealed in letters written to Zipp from friends, acquaintances, strangers, and peers.

Zipp probably wrote as many letters as he did sports columns in the newspapers. We have few letters written by him. Over the years many people wrote to Zipp just to say hello or to thank him for some kind word he had written. Many people wrote in response to his letters, or in reaction to something he wrote in his newspaper column. Some wrote simply to communicate with him because they sensed that he would appreciate hearing from them.

Celebrity status accrued to Zipp through his many years as a journalistic scribe and his affinity to be around people. People loved to read almost anything he wrote.

This study of Zipp Newman's life is a one-way trip. We have examined more than one hundred-seventy letters written to Zipp without having the benefit of reading either Zipp's initial letter to his correspondent, if indeed there was one, or a follow-up letter from Zipp. So, what do we find in these letters to Zipp?

The biographer of writer Henry James, Leon Edel, said during an interview that biography is irrelevant if no overlap is discovered between what the person did and the life that made those achievements possible.[1] Edel's five-volume biography of James assessed many unpublished letters written and received by James. Other documents were assessed as well.

Our assessment of Zipp Newman's life is based on letters he received from the 1920s to six days after his passing. Other documents in Zipp's history, and events in which he either planned or at least participated, help place him in the context of life in Birmingham, in Alabama, in the Southeast, and in American sports history.

The reader will understand clearly the overlap between Newman's life and his great achievements, as Leon Edel described the task of biography. Newman's achievements were made possible through his many relationships with people in different fields of endeavor.

Newman's book *The Impact of Southern Football*, published in 1969, is a mix of sports statistics and personal stories. He wrote about people who achieved various levels of greatness in sports, whether as an athlete, coach, or an administrator. In his book he wrote short biographies of twenty-one great achievers, from Paul "Bear" Bryant of the University of Alabama to Dr. Charles H. Herty, Dr. John J. Tigert, and Wallace Wade. Commissioners of the Southeastern and other conferences are lauded in his book for their contribution to Southern sports. Newman could not have written about these achievers had he not known them through his ability to make and keep honest relationships.

Taken chronologically, the content and tone of letters written to Newman transformed from projecting a professional and business-like character to recalling fond memories from decades past and thankfulness for long-term friendships. One cannot help but wonder whether the art of letter writing has lost its literary and personal powers in the twenty-first century, or whether it has been replaced by the ubiquity of email.

Henry Hardin "Zipp" Newman was a quiet person, never one to boast of his achievements, but quick in praise of others. His newspaper column "Dusting 'Em Off" revealed his character while he was writing about someone else. Indeed, from time to time he would write an article for *Coach and Athlete Magazine* about someone whom the world should never forget. That column was titled "Lest We Forget." We have placed excerpts of some of Zipp's articles in this biography, but mostly the letters received from admirers form the context of this book.

A sports editor at age twenty-five for *The Birmingham News*, Zipp used his writing skill and his love of sports to promote local charities or causes in need of financial assistance. His writing policy guided him to write only positively, according to his colleague Alf Van Hoose. Polio was the major national malady in the first quarter of the twentieth century, affecting many children. Leveraging his writing prowess and people's love of sports, Zipp would raise funds for that cause and several others, year after year. Never did he work these charities alone; he engaged the community and its civic and social organizations.

Newman's true character was never hidden from anyone. His is revealed in these letters from friends. Nothing in these letters as presented in this book is unrelated to the character of Henry Hardin Newman.

For more than three years, from conception to publication, Frances "Bee" Newman Morris (Zipp's daughter) and I have been working on this book. We believe that the reader will discern from reviewing the life of Henry Hardin "Zipp" Newman that he was certainly an excellent reporter and editor, a consensus maker, an organizer, a faithful husband and loving father. Not only was he a dreamer and creator of organizations and events, Newman was an institutional architect.

The reader will discover that Zipp Newman's work in his early years was full of excitement and high energy. His most productive years were from 1913 through 1959. The 1960s and beyond represented a change in Zipp's perspective. Those were the years of strengthening existing relationships and nurturing fading memories. Newspaper articles and letters written in the past are indispensable for recollection and Zipp had them in abundance. But he continued to create "written" memories for the future and to recollect them with his friends, as old men do, in his retirement.

Worth Earlwood Norman Jr
May 2019

---

[1] George Plimpton, ed., *Writers at Work: the Paris Review Interviews, Eighth Series* (New York, N.Y., U.S.A.: Penguin Books, 1988), 39.

Preface

When I was a child, I knew that my father was not only a famous person in our town, but a beloved man. It was not until I was in my teens that I began to realize the impact he had on other people and the community at large.

As the years passed, Henry Hardin "Zipp" Newman's life had influenced a broad spectrum of people in many different industries, skills, and expertise.

Three years ago, I talked with Worth E. "Woody" Norman, Jr. about helping me write a book about my father. It has taken time to complete this project and, I believe, it has been well worth the effort. Woody, not a Birmingham native, did not know who Zipp was, but as he read through our family albums and conducted research at the Birmingham Public Library and at Alabama Sports Hall of Fame, he came to recognize the obvious, positive impact my father had on people, not only locally but regionally and nationally.

Zipp Newman knew, it seems, every major sportswriter and broadcaster in the industry during his lifetime. People like Birmingham native Mel Allen, Red Barber, Bill Stern, and Lindsay Nelson. Zipp's book, *The Impact of Southern Football*, made its own impact on coaches, players, and journalists with an array of statistics and biographies. In his newspaper column he wrote fairly about the University of Alabama as well as Auburn University, and Kentucky's Centre College.

Much of this book uses letters written to Zipp from other people. Certainly, his newspaper articles are great sources of his journalistic skills, but we found that the letters written to Zipp show the world who he was and how he respected other people.

The reader will notice that our book is a narrative, moving chronologically through seven decades. The reader, therefore, can place Zipp within the timeline of history as events surrounding his life are recorded.

We hope you will enjoy reading about the life of Henry Hardin "Zipp" Newman.

Frances Newman Morris
May, 2019

1890s

Introduction

Long before Henry Hardin Newman became the famed southern sportswriter; before his family relocated from Henderson County, Kentucky to Birmingham, Alabama; even before he was born; one of his future-targeted college football teams played its first game.

The football program marked the beginning of the University of Alabama's thirty-three-year sports growth that seemed to reach its pinnacle in 1925.

On November 11, 1892 the University of Alabama played its first football game in Birmingham. It defeated another team, not a college, 56-0. Alabama was known then as the Crimson White and its first nickname was "The Thin Red Line.[1]

Three months later on February 22, 1893 the University of Alabama played another football game at Lakeview Park in Birmingham, before a crowd of five thousand spectators. The Alabama Polytechnic Institute at Auburn, Alabama fielded a team of players who overran their cross-state and future rival 32 to 22. The two schools played each other until 1907. That competition did not resume until 1948.[2] In 1893, on September 30, the University of Alabama admitted its first female student. Julia Tutwiler convinced UA's Board of Trustees to test a qualified form of co-education, to which they, along with a faculty committee, agreed. Updates or changes were in the wind.

A Happy Birthday

Henry Hardin Newman was born on May 24, 1894 in Smith Mills, Kentucky. Two years after Henry Hardin Newman's birth, the Supreme Court of the United States ruled on May 18, 1896, that segregation of the races in public facilities was legal. "Separate but equal" was the moniker placed on that ruling, an infamous decision that would not be overturned until 1954.

Newman's birth took place in the Commonwealth of Kentucky, whose title is held by only three other states – Virginia, Pennsylvania, and Massachusetts. Kentucky was a border state during the Civil War. Kentucky's sympathies, at first, were with the Confederacy but later switched toward the Union. Kentucky was a passthrough state for the Underground Railroad, routing former slaves into Ohio, primarily.

Smith Mills, located on the high ground above potential flooding of the Ohio River, is west of Louisville, south of Evansville, Indiana, and east of the Mississippi River by about fifty miles. The town has been referred to as "The Point" because of its elevation. Today Henderson County, Kentucky is considered by the United States Government as part of the Evansville (IN) Metropolitan [statistical] Area. Local people call their area Kentuckiana or the Tri-State Regions of Kentucky, Indiana, and Ohio.

The area around Henderson, Kentucky produced tobacco and in the mid-1800s most of its tobacco was exported to England. The settlement known as "The Point" was founded by William Roelosson and known for a while as "Roelosson's Settlement." Eventually the name Smith Mills took hold after its namesake Colonel Robert Smith. Smith served under General Andrew Jackson at the Battle of New Orleans in 1812. Eventually, the "s" was eliminated, and the town became Smith Mill.

Sports was and is part of Kentucky's self-identification. Zipp's grandfather Newman proudly boasted that one of his horses finished third in the Kentucky Derby. Zipp's uncles had blooded horses and ran with field trial dogs.[3]

---

[1] Michael Leo Donovan, *Yankees to Fighting Irish: What's Behind Your Favorite Team's Name* (Dallas: Taylor Trade Pub., 2004), 80.
[2] Alabama Department of Archives and History
[3] *The Birmingham News – Age Herald*. "So You Won't Talk, Eh, Mr. Newman?" by James Saxon Childers. April 4, 1937.

The 1890s

1900s

Introduction

The United States Census of 1900 for Henderson County, Kentucky provides an opening into understanding the family of Henry Hardin Newman. The magisterial district where the census was enumerated on June 26 was named Walnut Bottom. Henry Hardin Newman was only six years old. Eight years separated him from his next oldest sibling, Ab, age 14. A sister Beulah, 17, and brother Herbert, 15, comprise his other older siblings. Haynes, age 4, and Luther, less than one year, were the two youngest members of the family at the time of this census.[1]

Newman's father Henry, 43, is listed as head of household and employed as a clerk. Hettie, age 36, is the mother of the family. No occupation is listed for her. With the exception of Haynes and Luther, all members of the Newman family documented that they could read, write, and speak English. Occupations of other heads of household on the census sheet are day laborer; farm laborer; clerk; and a dry goods merchant named John Haynes.

Twenty years earlier, some of the occupations listed in Smith Mills included physicians and surgeons; a dealer in dry goods, groceries, boots, shoes and hats; two manufacturers of wagons, spring wagons, and buggies; and an undertaker.[2] Given the tobacco exporting business, the buggy manufacturing businesses, and Smith Mills' strategic location between the Ohio and Mississippi rivers, it appears that economic opportunities were available in this western Kentucky area. Why did the Newman family decide to relocate?

In 1900 Birmingham, Alabama recorded a population of 38,415. Founded after the end of the Civil War, Birmingham had its beginning as an incorporated municipality in 1871. Iron ore was discovered at Red Mountain and an economic boom developed rapidly. Steel companies headquartered in Ohio and Pennsylvania purchased land in and around the city and began their mining operations. News spread far and wide about the economically booming Birmingham and the high probability of employment. Perhaps this boom prompted the Newman family's relocation from Kentucky.

Former slaves and/or children of former slaves were hired to work the mines. A shortage of labor demanded that immigrants fill the work vacancies. There was, in the late 1800s, an influx of immigrants from Italy, Syria (Lebanon), and Ireland. Some historians have labeled Birmingham in the late 1800s and early 1900s as the "wild, wild west." It was a city out of control, but a city where economic opportunities seemed abundant. Business people in other parts of the nation and other parts of Alabama who could see what was happening in Birmingham, moved there to set up businesses: furnaces; restaurants; cat houses; law offices; various types of manufacturers and service industries.

Founded by dreamers in 1871, post-reconstruction to twentieth-century Birmingham had a labor problem. Historically dependent on agriculture, the former Confederate South lacked capital. Birmingham's leaders knew that with the discovery of iron ore mineral in the earth, fortunes could be made. But money, capital, had to be incoming and it was the North where funding for development was to be found. Thus, civic leaders embarked on massive promotions, citing Birmingham as part of the New South. Industrialization and urbanization were key to Birmingham's growth.

Over the years, pioneers such as John T. Milner, Frank Gilmer, Daniel Troy and James Sloss found interest in developing Birmingham. To them, Birmingham had great economic potential.

Many investors from the North began their long-term interest in what was known as the "Birmingham District." An economic upturn in the last quarter of the nineteenth century kept the engine working.[3]

The Birmingham News had its beginning on March 14, 1888 as *The Evening News*. By November 1889 the paper was known as *The Daily News*, and in 1896 *The Birmingham News*. It can be said that both the city and the *News* grew up together. Rufus Napoleon Rhodes founded the *News* and he was, perhaps, the city's biggest promoter.[4] Birmingham's founders and their successors knew that they had to attract capital investments to the area. Post-Reconstruction was of little to no help to the general population and it provided opportunities for the so-called Northern Carpetbaggers to exploit the remnants of the former Confederacy.

Historically, the Commonwealth of Kentucky was a mixed bag politically during and immediately following the American Civil War. A passthrough state for the Underground Railroad, Kentucky's political

The 1900s

ambiguities may have thwarted its economic growth. Still, it is difficult to determine with certainty why the Newman family decided to leave their old Kentucky home for Alabama.

Alabama has always produced notable and enterprising people. Future stage and movie actress Tallulah Brockman Bankhead was born in Jasper, Alabama, a town approximately forty miles northwest of Birmingham, on January 31, 1901 to a family of considerable political influence. A grandfather and an uncle were United States Senators representing Alabama. Tallulah's father, William B. Bankhead, served in the United States House of Representatives for eleven terms, the latter two terms as the House's forty-second Speaker. Tallulah's significance to sports in Alabama, however minor, would gather the attention of two sports enthusiasts years later.

The infamous *Constitution of the State of Alabama* was passed into law on December 1, 1901 during the administration of Governor William Jelks. Even into the twenty-first century, Alabama's 1901 Constitution is the most amended of the states in the nation. Admitted to the union on December 14, 1819, the State of Alabama celebrates its two-hundredth anniversary in 2019.

The *Louisiana Purchase Exposition* of 1904, also referred to as the *St. Louis World's Fair*, produced among other items, the ice cream cone. Birmingham's connection to the Fair is the cast-iron statue of the Roman god of fire and forge, *Vulcan,* which today overlooks Birmingham atop Red Mountain.

Since Birmingham's founding, the discovery of iron ore in Red Mountain set off a chain of events that resulted in the fast-growing iron and steel industry. Of note is the fact that none of the new industries in Birmingham were locally owned, except for the very small businesses.

Most of the rich mineral deposits in and around Birmingham were acquired by companies in the North and much political intrigue contributed to the subjugation of Southern mineral rights to Northern absentee landowners. Holdover post-reconstruction domination by the North accounted for most of the legal acquisition of the mineral rights, and not without the assistance of the United States Government.

The Newman family relocated to Birmingham, Alabama sometime in 1906 with possibly a short stay in Columbia, Tennessee. Henry Hardin Newman (not yet known as "Zipp") was twelve years old and had probably seen a lot during his short life-span. A thin, lightweight boy, he was adept at running. His deep love of sports would emerge within six years of arrival in Birmingham. Sports, to most people, was a distraction from anything else negatively perceived, and was a welcomed diversion from daily life. Zipp's love of sports and his emerging understanding of life's daily struggles would develop in his thinking as two sides of the same coin.

Birmingham's need for skilled labor was in high demand when the Newman family settled in. The city had earned the name "Magic City" through its remarkable economic turnaround. The former "district" was growing, had gained a reputation for progress, and therefore attracted labor and investments. The Newman family, most likely, was attracted to Birmingham for its employment opportunities.

Young Henry Hardin Newman would develop his place in history in the Magic City, the Southeast, and nationally, in the not too distant future.

Though booming Birmingham had a salty reputation, its taming began in 1907. The October 29, 1907 edition of *The Birmingham News* headlined "The Prohibition Wave Sweeps Jefferson County." A majority of citizens voting in a special election effectively ousted more than one thousand eight-hundred saloons. Several saloons were located near steel mills, furnaces, and other factories associated with the iron and steel industry. Some of those saloons were owned by labor organizers and doubly functioned as gathering places for labor union meetings or union organizing efforts. The upstairs of some of those establishments maintained a type of entertainment business, complete with beds.[5]

On November 16, 1907 Hugh Roberts of the *Tuscaloosa News* first used the term *Crimson Tide* at the Alabama-Auburn football game, a 6-6 tie. That first football game between those two schools would be their last gridiron encounter until 1948. It would be the young, future sports reporter Zipp Newman who would pick up and promote the term *Crimson Tide* in much of his written work. Newman's continuous use of the moniker made *Crimson Tide* stick. Sports and sports reporting were in their start-up and expansion phases during the first decades of the twentieth century and Newman would create his niche.

The Birmingham News Building
Circa 1947

By 1909, Henry Hardin Newman, while in high school, was working for the *Birmingham News* for $2.00 per week. At one period he worked three local newspapers as a carrier. *The Birmingham News* office was then located at Third Avenue and Twenty-first Street; *The Birmingham Ledger* at the corner of Twenty-first Street and First Avenue; and the *Age-Herald* on Fifth Avenue between Twenty-first and Twenty-second Streets. Young Newman worked all three, most likely delivering the publications transported with a bicycle. His route took him to the other side of Red Mountain from downtown Birmingham in the area which would become Homewood, Alabama. It was uphill, literally, from Birmingham to Homewood.[6] Imagine riding a bicycle uphill loaded with newspapers and imagine the energy supplied by a skinny, young boy.

The City of Birmingham expanded in 1909 and annexed the towns or townships of Ensley, North Birmingham, Pratt City, and Woodlawn. The *Birmingham Terminal Station* was also built in 1909. A railroad center, the city was served by seven different railroads. Six of those railroad companies funded the building of the architecturally Byzantine structure.[7] Sixty years later the terminal was razed as automobiles and air travel superseded train travel. But by the 1960s Birmingham was on a steady pace to replace Mobile and Montgomery as Alabama's lead city.

Aviation pioneers and brothers Wilbur and Orville Wright established a flight school in 1909 on what is now the site of Maxwell Air Force Base in Montgomery, Alabama, six years after their inaugural flight at Kitty Hawk, North Carolina.

Alabama was an interesting and growing state at the beginning of the twentieth century. But it was Birmingham and its leadership who envisioned a transformation from an agriculture-based economy into an

The 1900s

industrial powerhouse. The United States as a nation was also coming into its own internationally and would be tested in the not too distant future. But with Birmingham's growth there came with it supporting industries, collateral businesses, and multiple niches of opportunities for corporate and personal development. Newspapers played the major communication role in reporting on and developing the city and its fast-changing culture.

---

[1] 1900 United States Census, Henderson County, Kentucky, Magisterial district #8, Walnut Bottom, enumerated on June 27, 1900, enumerator Clyde Grady

[2] http://hendersonkyhistory.com/SmithMillsHist.htm

[3] Henry M. McKiven, Jr. *Iron and Steel: Class, Race, and Community in Birmingham, Alabama 1875-1920.* (Chapel Hill: The University of North Carolina Press, 1995), 55-75.

[4] The Birmingham News Company. *The Mirror of Our Times: The Birmingham News – More Than a Company.* Birmingham: The Birmingham News Company, 1997. Taken from article authored by Marlene Rikard.

[5] *The Birmingham News.* "The Prohibition Wave Sweeps Jefferson County." October 29, 1907.

[6] *The Birmingham News – Age Herald.* "So You Won't Talk, Eh, Mr. Newman?" by James Saxon Childers. April 4, 1937.

[7] https://en.wikipedia.org/wiki/Birmingham_Terminal_Station

1910s

Introduction

Birmingham's population in 1910 had tripled over the previous decade to 132,685. The U.S. Census of 1910 provides an update of the Newman family.

The April 23, 1910 census of Jefferson County, Alabama (Birmingham) documented the Newman family as: Henry, 52, and head of household worked as a salesman in a dry goods store; his wife Hettie, 47; and children Herbert E., 25, worked in a railroad office; Beulah, 22[1]; Hardin [Zipp] was 15, just one month away from turning 16; Haynes, 13; Luther, 10; Lillian, 5, the newest member of the family since the census of 1900 in Henderson County, Kentucky. The family lived at 2412 Fourth Avenue in Birmingham. All family members were born in Kentucky. Hettie's parents were born in Virginia; Henry's parents in Kentucky.

The Newman family had three lodgers at the time of the 1910 census. Frank Larkins, 30, worked at the railroad station; Clarence Crawford, 21, was a railroad locomotive fireman. Both men were born in Alabama. Gordon Wills, 20, worked as an office clerk at a railroad company. He was born in North Carolina.

Other occupations recorded by neighbors of the Newmans were railroad conductor; fireman at City Hall; cash boy in a department store; manager of a typewriter shop; a restaurant worker; three nurses employed by private families; a special agent for Southern Express; five other people working for the railroad; two salesmen for a dry goods store; a postal clerk; and a stockbroker for an investment firm. Of the fifty names listed on the census sheet, all lived on Fourth Avenue. Their places of birth indicate a microcosm of a regional, cultural mix: Alabama, Georgia, Germany, Illinois, Ireland, Kentucky, Louisiana, Mississippi, and North Carolina.[2]

Birmingham, as had been cited by historians, was "baseball crazy" in the earliest years of the twentieth century. So, too, was the son of one of Birmingham's great industrialists, baseball crazy.

To get our historical bearings on sports history, the first baseball game in the United States is recognized as the June 19, 1846 encounter between the New York Nine and the Knickerbockers. The competition was played in Hoboken, New Jersey.[3] By contrast, the first recognized football game was played on November 6, 1869 in Brunswick, New Jersey.[4]

In 1881 in a frenzy of industrial development, J.H. and W.H. Woodward formed the Woodward Iron Company. On a plot of land twelve miles west of Birmingham, the brothers built their furnaces. Early in the 1900s when Birmingham was booming, Woodward and other steel industry companies teamed with the Tennessee Coal and Iron Company to expand production.[5]

Joseph H. (J.H.) Woodward first made his money in Ohio but when it was discovered that iron ore was packed inside Birmingham's Red Mountain, he purchased many acres of land for his new Alabama-based company, A.W. Woodward Company. Though not the same businessman as his father, Rick Woodward loved baseball and was determined to become a part of a baseball legacy. He built Rickwood Field. The name of the ball park was taken from his nickname "Rick" and the first half of his surname, "Wood." The young Woodward spent a lot of time and energy developing his Rickwood Field. He took his lead from the legendary Connie Mack.

Cornelius McGillicuddy was the manager and a part owner of the Philadelphia Athletics of the American League in the early 1900s. Known popularly as Connie Mack, he convinced Athletics' majority owner Ben Shibe to build a larger and better ballpark not of wood, but of iron and steel. Shibe Park opened April 12, 1909. Shortly after Woodward acquired the Birmingham Barons, he announced that he would build a ballpark.

Woodward visited Philadelphia and Mack. Mack took a liking to Woodward and traveled to Birmingham to tour the site where Woodward wanted to build his ballpark. Eventually Connie Mack assisted Woodward in the design and the construction of Rickwood Field, based on the design of Shibe Park in Philadelphia.[6]

The ballpark would become the longest-running, active professional baseball field in America. The big opening day was in 1910. Birmingham fully backed their team. Downtown merchants acquired tickets for employees and customers, and they closed shop at 12:00 noon in time for the afternoon game. Window shopping was probably the only shopping done that afternoon in downtown Birmingham.

First Baseball Game at Rickwood Field

On August 18, 1910 at Rickwood Field, the first baseball game was played. Henry Hardin Newman probably attended this first game with his father. The Birmingham Barons defeated the Montgomery Climbers 3-2 on a Thursday.[7] Zipp was sixteen years old and a newspaper carrier.

The following day at Rickwood Field was called "Suffrage Day." Female employees at Southern Bell Telephone Company played another female team from Bessemer. It was a one-inning exhibition game.[8] The Nineteenth Amendment to the United States Constitution, Women's Suffrage, would not become law until 1920. The point of the game was to bring attention to the proposed amendment, an admixture of sports and politics.

Football at Rickwood Field

Henry Hardin "Zipp" Newman, the former newspaper carrier, became in 1912 a sportswriter at *The Birmingham News*.[9] Zipp, like some other boys, would hang around the newspaper's sports department. He became an assistant to the assistant sports writer. His big break would come the following year.

Vanderbilt University and Auburn University developed successful, winning football seasons between the years 1900 and 1913. Both schools had excellent coaches, accruing excellent competitive records.

Mike Donahue made Auburn University (Alabama Polytechnic Institute) into a football powerhouse between 1904 and 1922. Born in County Kerry, Ireland, he played his collegiate career at Yale University.

Dan McGugin coached at Vanderbilt University from 1904 to 1934. In his first year, at age 24, the Vanderbilt football team was undefeated. McGugin, born in Iowa and called "Irish" from time to time, played his college days at the University of Michigan and became an All-America guard under head coach Fielding "Hurry-Up" Yost.

The 1913 football season for both schools was going well during the first half of the season. Auburn shut out their first six opponents with impressive scores. Vanderbilt blanked its first three competitors but had a big problem with its fourth – the University of Michigan. Played in

The 1910s

Nashville, McGugin's former coach Yost and the Wolverine team crushed the Commodores 33 to 2. It was the worst defeat endured by McGugin in all his time at Vanderbilt. Up until this time the game of the year was to be between Vanderbilt and Auburn.

On November 15, 1913, Zipp began his sportswriting career in earnest by reporting for *The Birmingham News* on the Auburn-Vanderbilt football game, a game played at Rickwood Field. It was to be a critical game. By this time Auburn was still undefeated and Vanderbilt had already lost two games. But Vanderbilt had defeated its in-state rival Tennessee the week before, which gave momentum to a potential upset in the game with Auburn.

Rickwood Field
Birmingham, Alabama

The two football powerhouses were well coached by the two men of Irish descent. Auburn won the encounter 14 to 6. Newman, who had earned the nickname "Zipp" for being the first high school runner in Alabama to complete the 100-yard dash in 10 seconds flat, was now on his way to pursuing his dream of being a sportswriter.[10] His sportswriting career would be a defining influence on the development of sports reporting across the region and the nation. But other interests grew out of his altruistic character and thinking. Zipp believed that sports was not simply a distraction from the daily grind of life. He sensed that sports could be leveraged, positively changing the grind of life. How did this attitude develop?

Family members have said that Zipp's father was somewhat of an attraction to people or at least a magnet drawing people to his home. People came to Henry, Sr. for help. Some believe that Henry acted as an apothecary and provided a level of medical help to people in need. This phenomenon was a weekly if not a daily occurrence. As a teenage boy Zipp would have noticed his father's altruistic character.

The 1910s

It must be said, however, that no documentary evidence underwrites this understanding of the family patriarch as a medical person. Regardless of the lack of evidence, Zipp was affected by his father's selflessness.[11]

On July 28, 1914 war broke out in Europe and would become a world war until it ended on November 11, 1918.

In 1916 the United States suffered a massive outbreak of polio, a situation that would cause Zipp Newman to involve himself a few years later. Polio affected children, primarily. Polio was the most devastating disease of that era.

On October 18, 1916, in the Birmingham suburb of Irondale, a 5.1 magnitude earthquake shook Jefferson and Shelby counties. It remained for many decades the strongest earthquake measured in the State of Alabama.

Civitan International, a service organization, was founded in Birmingham in 1917 by Courtney Shropshire, a medical doctor. A native of New Orleans, Shropshire eventually relocated to Birmingham after graduating from Johns Hopkins University and the Mayo Clinic. He joined a local Rotary Club in 1917 but determined that it was too centered on enhancing the businesses of its members rather than the community at large. He founded *Civitan* as an organization serving individual and community needs, with citizenship, and with emphasis on helping people with developmental disabilities.[12]

In addition to its love of sports, Birmingham and its civic leaders would become associated with philanthropy by generating multiple social safety-net outreach programs. Newman would not be a minor player in philanthropy.

College football experienced some unique events in 1917. On September 29, according to a letter written in 1972 from Tony Ulrich to Zipp, there was a football doubleheader: Georgia Tech v Furman 25-0; Georgia Tech v Wake Forest 33-0. Those were the first two games of the season for Georgia Tech who was then named the *Golden Tornado,* and its coach in his fourteenth year was John Heisman.[13] This is the type of information Newman loved to collect. Newman loved statistics. The more detail, the better. It was an exciting time.

Tony Ulrich was custodian and director of the Dick Lamb Football Collection. He called his organization the Football Information Bureau and it was located in Dayton, Ohio. Newman and Ulrich shared a common interest in sports statistics and in sports oddities like the football doubleheaders. Their shared interests forged a strong personal relationship over the years.

The Irony of Zipp Newman's Military Service

On June 24, 1918 Zipp was inducted into the new National Army, as it was then called. He served from June 24 to August 11, 1918 in the 43rd Casualty Company and from August 11, 1918 to February 12, 1919 Newman served at the Base Hospital in Camp McClellan.

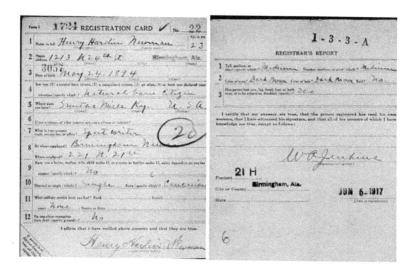

Henry Vance, Zipp's managing editor at *The Birmingham News*, wrote about Newman's departure for the Army. The headline read: ZIPP NEWMAN JOINS UNCLE SAM'S FORCES; LEAVES JUNE 24 FOR CAMP. The sub-headline tells the story: "After Several Unsuccessful Attempts to Volunteer, Sport Writer Is Called for Service." In other words, after attempts at volunteering to enlist in the military – and being rejected for health reasons – the Army drafted Newman when "push came to shove" during the War.

Not quite five years after Zipp's first sportswriting assignment at the 1913 Auburn-Vanderbilt football game, Vance wrote, "But for the fact that there might be a stranger in town there would be no necessity of saying Zipp 'who.' For almost everybody in Birmingham knows Zipp." The young 24-year old Assistant Sporting Editor, it appears, had already made his mark. Certainly, he made an impression on Henry Vance. Newman was scheduled to depart on June 24 for Camp Sevier near Greenville, South Carolina. Sevier was a temporary military site or cantonment for the purpose of training National Guard soldiers for service in World War I. The camp was established in July 1917. Training included a range of military skills such as artillery instruction, infantry training, gas defense and how to use a machine gun. By the end of the war more than 100,000 soldiers had been trained at Camp Sevier and with the signing of the armistice on November 11, 1918 the camp was designated as a demobilization center. Camp Sevier was closed as a military training project on April 8, 1919.

Army Private Henry Hardin Newman
Probably at Camp Sevier, South Carolina

On July 4, 1918 Zipp was not stationed at Camp Sevier, although he might have been for a few days. He was on the surgical operating table at Camp Pike in Little Rock, Arkansas. According to a newspaper article, a Birmingham soldier stationed at Camp Pike, Byrd Haley, told *The Birmingham News* about Zipp's surgery which had taken place on July 4 to correct a minor physical defect.

It is ironic that Zipp's "minor physical defect," a condition that precluded his volunteering for the National Army, was corrected by the Army after the young reporter was drafted into service.

Zipp was honorably discharged from *The United States Army* on February 12, 1919 at Camp McClellan, Anniston, Alabama, having served two hundred thirty-four days.[14] His discharge papers indicated that his rank was Private First Class; that he had not qualified as a rifle

The 1910s

marksman; nor had he mounted a horse, and that he had no battle engagements, skirmishes, or expeditions. His physical condition at the time of discharge is described as good and his character as "Very Good."[15]

[1] Beulah Newman age is incorrect either on this census or in the 1900 census.

[2] 1910 United States Census, Jefferson County, Alabama, Enumeration District 183, January 16, 1920, City of Birmingham, Enumerator Mrs. Bessie Bryant.

[3] https://www.hobokenbaseball.com/

[4] https://scarletknights.com/sports/2017/6/11/sports-m-footbl-archive-first-game-html.aspx

[5] McKiven, *Iron and Steel*, 12, 98.

[6] Timothy Whitt. *Bases Loaded with History: The Story of Rickwood Field – America's Oldest Baseball Park*. (Birmingham: The R. Boozer Press, 1995), 21-21.

[7] Black, Art. *Rickwood Field*

[8] Allen Barra, *Rickwood Field: a Century in America's Oldest Ballpark* (New York: W.W. Norton & Company, 2010), v.

[9] Alabama Department of Archives and History

[10] Newman, Zipp. *The Impact of Southern Football*. (Montgomery: Morris-Bell Publishing Company, 1969), xv.

[11] A document titled "Personal Notes" found in the Morris family papers appears to be a five-page resume of Newman. It is not dated but elements mentioned within the document suggest that its date is 1949 or 1950. It reads like a nomination form from page four to the end. Page One contains an interesting paragraph: *His [Newman's] father was a small town druggist. As a child, Zipp hung around his father's drug store and saw all the sick and ailing who came there for aid. This made a great impression on him, and no doubt in later life influenced him in his fine humanitarian work.*

[12] https://en.wikipedia.org/wiki/Civitan_International

[13] https://en.wikipedia.org/wiki/1917_Georgia_Tech_Golden_Tornado_football_team

[14] U.S. Army Circular 106 W.D. dated December 3, 1918 provided the rationale for discharging enlisted men at the conclusion of World War I. The circular number is referenced on Newman's discharge certificate.

[15] Honorable Discharge from The United States Army, Camp McClellan, Anniston, Alabama, February 12, 1919.

1920s

Introduction

The population of Birmingham grew more than twenty-eight percent to 178,806 between the years 1910 and 1920,[1] giving the city a weight of importance that would propel its leadership throughout the state and the Southeast.

Henry Hardin "Zipp" Newman resumed his sportswriting position at *The Birmingham News* shortly after his discharge from the Army in 1919 and within weeks he became the newspaper's sports editor at the retirement of Henry Vance. Zipp was, at age twenty-five, the youngest sports editor of a major publication in the South. Newman had established himself in sportswriting prior to his service in the military. It was now time to develop and grow as America recovered from the war.

In 1920 *The Birmingham News* acquired *The Birmingham Ledger*, thereby not only expanding its local readership but making it a significant journal across the Southeast. As an experienced sportswriter Zipp was in a good if not excellent position to become the leading sports journalist not only in Birmingham but in the region.

One of the first people to send good wishes to Zipp on his promotion was the President of the *Southern Association of Baseball Clubs*, John D. Martin:

> "I note that you have succeeded Henry Vance as sports editor of the Birmingham News, and I want to sincerely congratulate you upon obtaining this position, which I know you are fully competent to fill."[2]

This letter, indicative of outside recognition of Zipp's skill in sports journalism, gave evidence of a professional relationship already in place between the two men.

Zipp, unmarried, was living with his family at home. The 1920 United States Census provides interesting pieces of information about Zipp's family and how people lived during that decade. Henry, 62, Zipp's father, was listed as working in sales in a clothing store; Hettie, 56, his mother, was homemaker; Zipp was listed as Hardin H., 25, sports editor, newspaper; J. Haynes, 23, a fireman on a locomotive; Luther, 21, fireman with a railroad; and sister Lillian, 14. The Newmans had boarders, as many families did at that time. Frank Larkins, 35, a boarder, was chief clerk at an auto store, and William Hendricks, 28, was an editor at *The Birmingham News*. The home address listed for the Newman family was 1201 25th Street North, Birmingham.[3] Frank Larkins was also listed in the 1910 census, showing an age of 30. One of the two census data sheets had to be incorrect, because Larkins was a boarder with the Newman family for at least ten years.

The fact that William Hendricks and the other boarders were not living on their own indicates how difficult the times were on building a firm, personal, financial base. Hendricks and Zipp, undoubtedly, shared their journalistic discoveries not only between themselves but throughout the entire boarding house.

There might have been an accommodation of time and space in the Newman household. Working hours may have varied greatly. Newspaper journalists must meet daily deadlines for publication. A newspaper with several editions per day would work several deadlines for its writers. Zipp and Hendricks might have worked at different shifts, so to speak, at The Birmingham News. Therefore, they might not have interacted at work or at home.

Regardless, there had to be accommodations made in the household, as well as rules. Times seemed to be simpler in the 1920s, but the complexity of living with many different persons requires restraint. Rules provided order; restraint required high personal character. Both are fundamental to relationship building.

On May 24, 1920, Zipp Newman turned twenty-six-years old, and four years earlier an outbreak of polio began to spread across the United States. Affecting mostly children, polio also affected adults. One such adult was Franklin Delano Roosevelt. Though not yet President of the United States, Roosevelt contracted polio at age thirty-nine in 1921.[4] No area of the United States was immune from this outbreak and it would soon hit Alabama; and even though Zipp Newman was a sports journalist, he would assume a leadership position in community service, particularly in fighting polio. He was learning how to leverage sports, beginning with developing relationships with as many people as possible. His relationship development, it appears, was to him not a task. It was second nature.

During that first assignment, reporting on the Auburn-Vanderbilt football game of 1913, Zipp met with and interviewed both coaches – Mike Donahue and Dan McGugin. Ten years later McGugin would be offered the head football coaching position at the University of Alabama. "Instead of accepting the offer, McGugin sold Alabama on taking his line coach Wallace Wade."[5] The University of Alabama then hired Wade, who succeeded coach Xen Scott.

Zipp Newman reported on all teams around the nation and not just those in the Southeast. The strongest and most successful, and most well-known, teams were in the Northeast, Midwest, and on the Pacific coast. Southern teams like Alabama, Vanderbilt, Auburn, Clemson, and Tennessee did not garner much national attention. Although Newman's favorite sport was baseball, his journalism developed mostly around covering and reporting on college football.

The Nineteenth Amendment granting voting rights to women was ratified on August 18, 1920.[6] It was ten years earlier, less one day, that the "Suffrage Day" baseball game was played at Rickwood Field between female teams from Bell South Telephone Company and workers from the nearby town of Bessemer, Alabama.

A United States Judge for the Northern District of Illinois, Kenesaw Mountain Landis, on November 12, 1920 became the first commissioner of major league baseball. Landis served in this capacity until November 25, 1944. He ruled baseball with an iron hand following the Black Sox scandal. Zipp Newman, Judge Landis, and a disgraced major league baseball pitcher would cross paths in the future.

Radio station WAPI began its on-air broadcasting in Birmingham in 1922. Its call letters attributed to Alabama Polytechnic Institute (API), later Auburn University.

Newman wrote to John D. Martin of the *Southern Association of Baseball Clubs* on January 7, 1924, apparently extolling the sportsmanship not only of the Birmingham-based Southern League but the Southern Association as well. Martin replied on January 10, writing:

The 1920s

"I appreciate more than I can say, the expression of your good will, which I certainly reciprocate. There is not a better delegation of honest-to-God sportsmen in the whole country than the Birmingham Southern League [the Southern Association was known as the Southern League from 1901 to 1919] gang, in which I include your good self."

Zipp had made inquiry about the umpire staff for the 1924 season. Martin replied that he had already mailed out contracts to nine men, believing that all of them would sign. However, he wanted to withhold that information until all contracts were in so that he could make a blanket public announcement. Martin then wrote "confidentially" that there would be two changes in the staff and then named them.[7] Zipp, the sports reporter and official scorer for baseball games played in Birmingham, had the confidence of the President of the Memphis-based organization of southern semi-professional baseball.

On April 12, 1924 Zipp received a letter from Martin stating that

"This is a most official letter to notify you of your reappointment as official scorer at Birmingham for the season of 1924, upon the nomination of that sterling democrat, the Hon. W.D. Smith."

Martin told Zipp that when he came to Birmingham the following week to watch the Birmingham Barons play, he expected to "swap a chew of tobacco" with Barons owner Rick Woodward.[8] Newman, as official scorer in Birmingham, would be sent the "scorer's dope" in a separate mailing from the association's statistician Irwin Howe.

Letters, and probably telephone calls to a lesser extent, were the primary means of communication. Of course, in the arena of sports the many face-to-face meetings were of high value. The renewal of friendships, the swapping of stories, recollection of past meetings, games and outings; these were the "infrastructural" items utilized not only to report sporting events to the public but for creating friendships.

The 1924 University of Alabama football team rolled through its first seven games, shutting out six of those teams with lopsided scores. Only Kentucky in the seventh game was able to place seven points against Alabama's forty-two. But it was the eighth game, a game in which Alabama was shut out that ended some of the season's hope. That game was played on Saturday, November 15, 1924, at Rickwood Field in

Birmingham. A letter dated November 16 and handwritten on the stationery of *The Dinkler Hotels* was addressed to the "Sports Editor of the Birmingham News."

Citing the "Good Book" the letter writer recalled that of a group of ten men who received great benefit, only one returned to express gratitude and praise. This was a letter of gratitude from a regional college president whose football team on the previous day defeated the powerful University of Alabama team 17-0. He closed his letter with:

> "... I want on behalf of my boys – with whom I always make the trips – and on my own behalf, to express our appreciation of the generous praise and portrayal you have given of our team and to the 'personal mention' you have made of the different men."

The letter, penned stylistically, was written by R. Ames Montgomery, the President of Centre College of Danville, Kentucky.[9]

Zipp Newman as a sportswriter and editor most assuredly did his homework before the game was played between *Centre* and *Alabama*, and once in the press box viewing the game, he knew all the players from both schools and their past, on-field performances. A stickler for detail, Newman mastered the art of research. His policy was always to write in a positive manner. He reported on this important Saturday game in the Sunday issue of his newspaper. The *Centre College* president read Zipp's article while in his hotel room, which was in either the *Tutwiler* or the *Redmont Hotel*, both of which were *Dinkler* hotels. The character of Zipp's article caused the *Centre* president to waste no time and he handwrote his letter.

Zipp had contacts in New York City. He made it a practice to send Christmas cards every year to his journalistic peers; college presidents and administrators; ball club owners and managers; coaches and players; and to parents of athletes. Cullen Cain received one such card. Cain was the manager of the Service Bureau of the National League of Professional Base Ball Clubs. On January 3, 1925 Cain wrote to Zipp that though he sends very few cards himself he seldom acknowledges any. But in Zipp's case Cain said:

> "It was such a card as only a man of sentiment and thought and warm feelings would write and send. It might be termed a hand-clasp across the distance. It might also be termed as a brave gesture such

as a man only makes to a friend to assure him of his support, his confidence and his affection."[10]

Many letters in subsequent years would be exchanged between Cain and Newman, personal and business. But it was Newman who made the initiative with his letter writing, and in many instances Zipp received thankful replies.

Closer to home, the *University of Alabama* football team won all nine of its regular season games in 1925. Two of those games were with non-conference schools – *Union College* of Tennessee and *Birmingham-Southern*. Except for one, Alabama shut out their opponents by impressive margins. *Birmingham-Southern* was defeated by a score of 50-7. Wallace Wade was in his third year as head football coach at the University of Alabama.

Alabama defeated LSU, Georgia Tech, University of the South (Sewanee), Mississippi A&M, Kentucky, Florida, and Georgia. An impressive record even though southern colleges were still not considered up to the level of teams in the Northeast, Midwest, and West Coast.

Go Figure

Clark Shaughnessy was in his tenth year as head coach at Tulane University, another Southern Conference team, and had achieved an undefeated football season in 1925. Tulane won nine games but played to a 6-6 tie with Missouri.

Newman wrote in his book, *The Impact of Southern Football*, that it was *Tulane University*'s football team that received the first invitation for the 1926 Rose Bowl Game in Pasadena, California. But Shaughnessy and Tulane's administration declined the invitation and at Shaughnessy's urging prevailed upon the Rose Bowl committee to invite Wallace Wade's *University of Alabama* team.[11] This turn of events was significant, unheard of, and puzzling. So, the University of Alabama football team and Zipp began preparing for the annual bowl game. The reporting of the 1926 Rose Bowl game would be a breakout moment for Zipp.

The *University of Alabama* Crimson Tide would play the *University of Washington* Huskies, a team that had a season record of 10-0-1. This was the first time that a southern football team competed in the annual Rose Bowl Game, which was Alabama's first bowl game. Two fortunate men would be at the same game.

Wallace Wade was doubly lucky or fortunate. Not only did Dan McGugin turn down Alabama's offer to leave Vanderbilt, he also recommended that Alabama hire Wade. Three years later, and for whatever reason, Tulane's Shaughnessy turned down the Rose Bowl invitation, favoring instead Wallace Wade's Alabama team. Zipp Newman was the other lucky man.

Newman documented the first half of the match-up between the Crimson Tide and Huskies, and then at half-time, he was asked by NBC radio to provide his analysis of the game's first two quarters. Zipp's on-the-spot analysis attracted national acclaim for his clarity. And much would be made of his analysis as the days and weeks went by. But his 2,300-word report in *The Birmingham News* on January 2, 1926 opened with nothing less than literary hyperbole:

> PASADENA, Calif., Jan. 2 -- Memories of the devastating 1906 earthquake which all but destroyed the city of San Francisco swept through the frenzied minds of 50,000 spellbound spectators here New Year's Day when the plunging, ruthless Crimson Tide of Alabama hurled the Purple Tornado of Washington far out into a dizzy sea.

> The whole Pacific coast cringed, while the Middle West and East trembled from the shock of a tidal wave that came after being disturbed by a vicious tornado. A Southland swept into its own as Alabama came from behind to score a 20-to-19 victory over Washington in the South's greatest intersectional football victory.[12]

Newman's dramatic and selective play-by-play narrative of the salient actions of the game brought home to the reader the grandiose victory achieved by the team from the South. It was not until years later, in 1937, that James Saxon Childers wrote that Newman, while appearing to be calm and cool in the press box with sports reporters from around the nation, was actually squirming inside, not sure whether the Crimson Tide would pull out the win.

Childers and other reporters of *The News* listened as Newman told his story.

> "In the first half Washington scores twice and failed to kick goal both times. It looked as if we [University of Alabama football team] were

in for a slaughter. And there I say. I was all huddled down in one corner of the press box, feeling as if I wanted to be anywhere but where I was. All these correspondents from the great newspapers of the country were sitting there making cracks about Alabama and wondering why the committee had invited a little Southern hick school to come play a great team like Washington. They kept asking me. And I couldn't tell them. I felt miserable."[13]

That Rose Bowl Game of 1926 launched the football legacy of the University of Alabama, the coaching credibility of Wallace Wade, and the popularity of sports reporter Zipp Newman.

Later in the year, on November 9, 1926, the U.S. Naval Academy Midshipmen football team played a double-header, a rarity. Navy defeated Drake 24-7 and Richmond 26-0. There have been no college football double-headers since. Tony Ulrich told this bit of trivia to Zipp in a 1972 letter.[14]

Zipp's newspaper and magazine articles of events and people cause people to react with their letters to Zipp. On April 7, 1927 Wil Paterson penned a letter to Zipp (written on *Rosemont Gardens* stationery, Montgomery, Alabama) about the kind words written about his brother James "Jim" Porter Paterson. Their father, William Burns Paterson, created *Rosemont Gardens* in 1890 and his children and their children had continued their floral business for more than one hundred twenty-five years. Why did Paterson send this letter to Newman?

Jim Paterson died at a relatively young age on April 4, 1927 and Newman wrote an article in tribute. Jim Paterson's brother Wil handwrote the letter to Zipp thanking him for such a kind remembrance saying,

> "He loved you and enjoyed you because you appreciated him. Your thoughtfulness and sympathetic kindness has [sic] made it easier for us to bear. It is just such a heart that you have shown that brings the world closer to the brotherhood of man. Haygood, Wallace, my dear sister Annie and Jim's dear wife join me in thanking you again."[15]

The Marriage of Zipp to Mary Frances

Henry Hardin Newman and Frances McNeil obtained their marriage license on June 6, 1927, witnessed by J.E. Dillard, pastor of Southside Baptist Church.[16]

Frances McNeil Newman
Image – *The Birmingham News*

Mrs. Perry McNeil sent invitations to several people requesting their presence at the wedding and marriage ceremony of her daughter Mary Frances McNeil and Henry Hardin Newman. It was an evening wedding on a Tuesday at 8:00pm at Southside Baptist Church.[17]

The sports department at *The Birmingham News* did its share of reporting on the marriage of "the Boss" and his bride. In a sense, the sports page was the social page for this event.

Frank Smith, Jr.'s column headlined "NEWS SPORTS EDITOR MARRIES MISS MCNEIL – *Zipp Takes The Count At Big Wedding In Southside Baptist Church*." He wrote that,

> "There were probably more referees, headlinesmen, umpires and other officials present at the wedding than Zipp had ever seen before at one time. Nobody went out on strikes and there were no penalties for offsides or holding. The game was perfectly played through every detail. The altogether charming lady who consented to join up with Zipp is Miss Frances McNeil. That they will make a darned swell pair will be guaranteed by anyone who knows them."[18]

The article continued, saying that the church was well-decorated with "choicest buds and blooms" lavishly used from *Rosemont Gardens*.[19] Now we see a connection. The Montgomery, Alabama Paterson family who thanked Zipp for his kind article years earlier, provided the floral arrangements for the wedding.

Zipp's best man was Karl Landgrebe. It is not known how the two men met but Landgrebe came to Birmingham in 1910. He was an iron and steel executive with the Tennessee Coal, Iron & Railroad Company (TCI). A native of Cleveland, Ohio, Landgrebe graduated from the Case School of Applied Science. It is probable that sports was the glue that brought them together and their relationship had to have been solid since Zipp asked Landgrebe to be best man at his wedding.

Landgrebe started baseball and soccer teams at his company, the soccer team winning the Ramsay Cup in 1919 and 1920. His baseball team at Tennessee Coal was regarded as one of the best semi-pro teams in the nation. Another connection might have been through Rick Woodward, the owner of the Birmingham Barons. Landgrebe was also a director and member of the Woodward Golf and Country Club.[20]

It did not take long for congratulatory letters to come. Dan McGugin wrote on June 11, 1927 that he had just heard that Zipp was "tied up." "I congratulate you and the lady most heartily." Sensing he was late in his acknowledgement, McGugin wrote that he had better send Frances and Zipp some bacon and eggs which would be handy. No longer coaching at Vanderbilt, McGugin was practicing law full time in Nashville, Tennessee.[21]

The marriage of Newman to Miss McNeil would flourish. The couple would have two daughters and a new home. The Birmingham area would continue to grow and Zipp Newman, as an acclaimed sports reporter, would take his place in the region's popularity.

The *Alabama Theater* opened in Birmingham on December 26, 1927. It was the flagship of a chain of theaters owned by Paramount Corporation. It would become a centerpiece of the arts in Birmingham. It is still in operation today.[22]

In 1928, Alabama's Convict Lease system ended, inaugurating a significant change in how the State of Alabama and the private coal industry operated. Local county sheriff offices raised money by leasing jailed personnel to coal companies to work in the mines. Treatment of inmates by private companies was often more brutal than that of the state. The curtailment of this project was one step in the right direction.[23]

The following year, the *Crippled Children's Clinic* was formed. The clinic was formed to treat polio.

"Children came from around the state, hundreds more than anticipated- and none were turned away. In the worst economic conditions in history, Birmingham opened its heart and its pocketbook to those less fortunate.

Initial plans were to treat about 25 children but by January 1930 more than 100 applications for children needing treatment were on file at the clinic. As the patient load grew, contributions miraculously kept pace with the increasing needs of the clinic. And more uncommon approaches to fund-raising were pressed into service."[24]

Ten years later Birmingham's *Monday Morning Quarterback Club* would be formed. Initially intended to review and analyze the weekend's football games, it also took on a philanthropic direction in support of the Crippled Children's Clinic.

The Great Depression hit on October 24, 1929 with its devastating stock market crash. It was the beginning of a terrible decade of recovery and it was a hopeful time of discovery. Zipp Newman, the well-established sports editor of a major newspaper in the Southeast, a reporter of details of significant sporting events, would develop a method to assist fans, primarily, to understand the game of football. His effort would receive informative responses.

[1] Alabama Department of Archives and History timeline
[2] John D. Martin. Letter. April 12, 1920. President, Southern Association of Baseball Clubs, Memphis, Tenn.
[3] 1920 United States Census, Jefferson County, Alabama, Enumeration District 55, April 23, 1910, City of Birmingham, Enumerator William Rhudy.
[4] https://amhistory.si.edu/polio/howpolio/fdr.htm
[5] *Coach & Athlete* magazine, volume 28, 1965, 42.
[6] https://www.ourdocuments.gov/doc.php?flash=false&doc=63
[7] John D. Martin letter, January 10, 1924
[8] John D. Martin letter, April 12, 1924
[9] Montgomery Ames letter, November 16, 1924
[10] Cullen Cain letter, January 3, 1925
[11] Newman. *Impact*, 153.
[12] *The Birmingham News*, reprint, December 28, 2016. Creg Stephenson.
[13] James Saxon Childers, "So You Won't Talk, Eh, Mr. Newman." *The Birmingham News*, Sunday April 4, 1937.
[14] https://en.wikipedia.org/wiki/1926_Navy_Midshipmen_football_team
[15] Wil Paterson letter, April 7, 1927
[16] Marriage License dated June 6, 1927, affidavit on June 7, 1927 by probate judge Robt. Hewitt
[17] Wedding Invitation by Mrs. Perry McNeil
[18] Frank H. Smith, Jr. *The Birmingham News*, June 1927, "News Sports Editor Married Miss McNeil."
[19] Jerry Bryan. "Dusting 'Em Off" *The Birmingham News*

---

[20] E.W. Barrett, ed. "Karl Landgrebe" in *Men of the South: A Work for the Newspaper Reference Library* (New Orleans: Southern Biographical Association, 1922), 76.

[21] Dan McGugin letter dated June 11, 1927, written on letterhead "McGugin, Evans & Catel" law firm

[22] https://www.bhamwiki.com/w/Alabama_Theatre

[23] Douglas A. Blackmon, *Slavery by Another Name: The Re-Enslavement of Black Americans from the Civil War to World War II* (New York: Anchor, 2009)

[24] https://www.mmqbc.org/

The 1920s

1930s

Introduction

At 259,678 Birmingham's population grew forty-five percent over the decade. Zipp and Mary Frances Newman were living at 1221 17th Street in Birmingham when the census for 1930 was enumerated. Taken on April 23, the makeup of the recorded neighborhood is interesting. Not all residents were Alabama natives.

The Newmans' immediate neighbors were from Massachusetts, South Carolina, Tennessee, Missouri, Georgia, Mississippi, Kansas, the Irish Free State, and there was a family of Yiddish-speaking Russian Jews. There was a second family whose head-of-household was born in Russia. She was a mother of five adult sons, all born in Alabama, each working as a salesman. Three worked for an army surplus store and two worked at the Wooden Ware Company. The census shows that the sons' father was born in Russia.

Employment of the neighbors varied. Zipp was not the only neighborhood resident working at the newspaper. One of the Yiddish-speaking sons worked in circulation; his father, the head-of-household, was a buyer of cattle. [1] And the baseball craziness of Birmingham had not diminished. One of its greatest baseball moments would occur early in this decade.

Dixie Series and Dizzy Dean

The Depression years seemed not to interrupt certain activities, especially sports. The biggest sporting event of the early 1930s was the minor league Dixie Series played at Rickwood Field. The biggest name in baseball in 1931 was Dizzy Dean, a flamboyant pitcher for the Houston Buffaloes.

The series pitted the Houston Buffaloes of the Texas League against the Southern Association's Birmingham Barons. Everyone knew that

Dean and his Houston team would dominate the series. Birmingham's "baseball crazies" supported their Barons from the opening of Rickwood Field to present day. But those crazies craved the opportunity to witness the notorious minor league pitching star, Dizzy Dean, on their home field.

Even while in the minors, Dean could not keep his mouth shut. A braggart and a predictor of almost any future event, Dean knew not only how to pitch a baseball, but he also knew how to pitch to a crowd. And Birmingham fans could hardly wait to see Dean in this Dixie Series.

Zipp, knowing that the series would be dominated not by the Houston team but by none other than the magnanimous personality Dizzy Dean himself, wrote to a Houston colleague,

> "Wire me 150 words every day on Dizzy Dean. What does he do to pass the time? What does he eat? Let's have all the dope. He's started a stampede here for tickets. His name has already become a household word in Birmingham. From what you hear, you would think he's the whole Houston ball club.[2]

Not a moment to waste, Zipp gathers details – any detail. The question of the day was "What will Dizzy do in the series?" The answer was "pack Rickwood Field."

According to sportswriter and author Allen Barra, the Dixie Series was the top event in all of the South. There was almost nothing else like it in the entire nation. Dixie Series games prior to the 1931 event set Birmingham and all of Alabama on fire.

On the morning before the Dixie Series, September 15, 1931, Zipp wrote,

> "People will watch Dizzy Dean today who've never seen a baseball game ..."[3]

The match between the teams' two pitchers would either confirm young Dizzy Dean's prediction of a win, or it would send Dean into obscurity, as Dean himself described it. And so, in the first game of the series, matching the young Dean against a much older Ray Caldwell, Dean lost the game 1-0.[4] Zipp wrote the day after, that Dean deserved credit "for 10,000 of that crowd ..."[5]

Barra, in his 2010 book *Rickwood Field,* cited a Newman article of September 24, 1931 which Zipp wrote after the two teams traveled to

Houston, "What have the stars in store for Diz? ..."[6] Dizzy Dean's future success in baseball seemed secure. Indeed, it was. The loss to the forty-one-year-old Baron's pitcher Ray Caldwell did not ruin Dean's future in baseball. Dean played in the major leagues for the St. Louis Cardinals, Chicago Cubs, and the St. Louis Browns. In 1934 fastball pitcher Dean won thirty games and led the "Gashouse Gang" St. Louis Cardinals to the National League pennant. His baseball career, however, was cut short by an injury to his left foot. Some years later Dizzy Dean became a television color commentator for Saturday baseball games with sidekick Pee Wee Reese of the Brooklyn Dodgers.

Southern Conference Experiences a Reordering

On December 8-9, 1932 the Southeastern Conference was established. At the annual meeting of the Southern Conference in Knoxville, Tennessee, the thirteen Conference schools located west and south of the Appalachian Mountains withdrew their Southern Conference membership and reorganized as the Southeastern Conference.[7] This was the beginning of what was to become one of the strongest college football conferences in the United States.

The Southern Conference experienced another set of college withdrawals in 1953 when the University of Virginia, Duke, North Carolina, North Carolina State, Clemson, Wake Forest, and Maryland formed the Atlantic Coast Conference.

Newman was familiar with the sports accomplishments of all of the colleges in the Southeast. Regardless of the shifting arrangements of schools into conferences, Zipp's interaction with the schools of the South was never interrupted. Football reporting was his major journalistic output, but baseball held high interest.

"Happy" Chandler

A.B. "Happy" Chandler was a multi-sport athlete while in college in Kentucky. Given his sports background, it is highly probable that he at least knew of Zipp Newman's sports columns and had probably met with him. Chandler held several state and federal elective offices in the Commonwealth of Kentucky. On December 12, 1932, Chandler wrote a letter to Zipp, typed on Inter-Southern Life Insurance Company stationery. In the area below the company name where an address is printed, two lines were blacked out, leaving only the City of Louisville,

The 1930s

31

Kentucky. Chandler's name and a trust company name were on the left side listed as "co-receivers."

Chandler used it to write to Zipp about their recent visit. He had been in Meridian, Mississippi and on his return to Kentucky stopped in Birmingham to visit with Newman. He mentioned how powerful a football team was the University of Alabama and lamented a bad season at the University of Kentucky. Kentucky had suffered through a 4-5 football season while Alabama enjoyed winning eight of its ten games.

At the time of this letter Chandler was Kentucky's Lieutenant Governor and at the front end of his illustrious career in politics and sports.

Zipp's Kentucky hometown of Smith Mill is five miles to the northwest of Corydon, Chandler's town of birth. Chandler wrote that he enjoyed his time with Zipp and was "Glad to learn you're a Henderson County [Kentucky] boy."[8]

Chandler did make a request of Zipp.

> "I wish occasionally, when you have endorsed any sports squibs that you know I would be interested in, that you would send them to me. Of course, I do not want to burden you too much with this sort of request, but I never have forgotten, and I still keep in my old scrap book, the story which you told about the 'Twelve Young Men Drunk on Lemonade who shot up Rickwood Field.'"

The relationship that developed between Newman and Chandler grew over the ensuing years. Given Zipp's sports reporting authority and Chandler's eventual appointment in 1945 as major league baseball's second commissioner following the death of Judge Kenesaw Mountain Landis, the two men would interact professionally for years to come.

Rick Woodward's Memoirs

Zipp Newman understood that men who achieved great success for the benefit of other people should have their story told. So Zipp asked Rick Woodward to write his baseball memoirs.[9] On January 29, 1934, Woodward wrote to Zipp,

Frances Newman Morris

"When I promised to write my recollections after twenty-four years, I failed to realize how difficult it would be, and what a test of friendship it really is. I have tried to do my best. We must let it go at that."[10]

Woodward's history would have to be written by others. Newman made his contribution. But Zipp also wanted to contribute more to the fans of football. Fans who did not necessarily understand the game.

The Late, Great Football Scoring Sheet

A working mind is never at rest. Newman's love of sports, particularly baseball, kept him in business. During his after-hours Zipp worked as the official scorer at all Birmingham Barons home games, a position assigned to him by the President of the Southern Association of Baseball. But it was the complexity of football which motivated Zipp to spin his wheels developing his famous, actually infamous, scoring sheet.

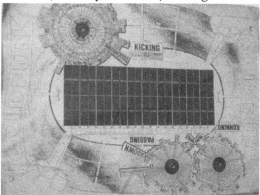

Zipp Newman's Grid Fun Game
It received as much popularity as did Zipp's football scoring sheet

Once perfected in his mind and written on paper, and copyrighted, Zipp mailed his invention to "those who would know" for commentary and feedback. The number of responses to his mailing was impressive, particularly considering the giants in the field of football coaching and sports reporting.

W.A. Alexander

The earliest dated response came from the head football coach at Georgia Tech, W.A. Alexander. The November 9, 1934, three-paragraph response, acknowledged first that he was happy to learn that Zipp would

The 1930s

33

be in Atlanta on November 17 to cover the Georgia Tech-Alabama game. Georgia Tech lost 40-0. It was Alexander's third paragraph where he gave a vague response to Zipp's inquiry about a starting player handicapped by influenza. Sandwiched in the middle, Alexander said that he expected that a "good many people will be interested in your football score sheet printed in the program."

A little more hopeful-sounding was the fact that Alexander said he would be glad to show the score sheet to Christy Walsh and his agency but punctuated by acknowledging, "... the first time I have an opportunity." His zinger, "I would advise that you mail him same."[11] Zipp had already sent his material to Christy Walsh.

Joseph Bihler

Joseph Bihler of the *The Christy Walsh Syndicate* wrote on November 22, 1934, "Regarding your two copyrights ... there is no doubt it would be useful ..." Bihler elaborated on three categories for Zipp to consider – FOR PROGRAMS; FOR RADIO; and FOR NEWSPAPERS. Bihler suggested that Zipp consider radio advertisers with national distribution. Bihler's advice came in seven paragraphs.[12]

Bihler's advice to Zipp was practical, because different channels employ different methods of distribution of advertising material. Zipp thought, initially, that his scoring sheet would be an item imbedded in a football game program for fans.

O.B. Keeler

O.B. Keeler of *The Atlanta Journal* wrote on November 21, 1934, "Your football chart is a swell idea ... it seems to me that it should be grabbed off promptly ..." Because Keeler and Newman were in the same business, he closed with,

> "I can use this sort of thing myself, in covering a football game and doing the subsequent story."[13]

Newman copyrighted his scoring sheet into two versions. One was for football spectators viewing a game from the stands. The other version was developed for radio listeners. Those documents were mailed to many sports-related recipients. Newman sought not only feedback on the scoring sheer – which he received in abundance – but assistance in its promotion, in which he received only advice.

The 1930s

Dan McGugin

Newman received two letters dated November 15, 1934, from former Vanderbilt University football coach Dan McGugin and Director of Athletics. In one of his letters McGugin acknowledged the usefulness of Zipp's two versions of the scoring sheet.

The other letter to Zipp offered help in promoting the scoring sheet. The remainder of his letter was in response to questions Zipp apparently asked about football's time clock. This was a technical question requiring an expert's opinion. McGugin wrote:

> "As to the Western Union time clock. This should be used as the official time. Formerly the headlinesman kept the time and then it was felt best for the field judge to be the time keeper. ... [During the last five minutes of a half] ... the stop watch of the field judge should be the official time ... The Western Conference went into this very carefully and this is the method that they use."[14]

Clearly the scoring sheet was not the only item on Zipp's mind. Ever exploring new ways to explain sports, Newman continued writing his column and producing new ideas.

Other Responses to the Scoring Sheet

H.D. Drew, University of Alabama Athletic Association wrote that "Your scoring system is great."[15]

C.A. Wynne, Director of Athletics, University of Kentucky wrote that Zipp's scoring sheet was something that has been needed. And, "thanks for your kind remarks."[16]

P.B. Parker, Director of Athletics, University of Tennessee wrote to Zipp "your scoring sheet will prove an important factor ..." "We are delighted to be able to connect up with Auburn for an annual appearance in Birmingham."[17]

Frank Thomas, Football Coach, University of Alabama: "Your sheet is a good system; will create interest; beneficial to public; for scouts; standardizes terminology ..."[18]

Harry Mehre, University of Georgia: "Studied your scoring sheet; good for fans; scouts; I congratulate you."[19]

Wallace Wade, Duke University, "Your scoring sheet is very helpful to me between the halves in diagnosing plays that took place in the first half …"[20]

Bernie Bierman, University of Minnesota, "Your [football scorings] sheet is good. It is complete while simple."[21]

An NBC Radio writer in San Francisco wrote to Zipp about several items including the scoring sheet and the Rose Bowl Tuscaloosa Elephants.[22]

E.P. Madigan, St. Mary's College-California, "Scoring system good, best regards."[23]

Edmond Armes, The Travelers, "studying your proposed scoring sheet. "It appeals to me as a spectator …"[24]

Ted Cox, Tulane University head football coach, "looking over your score sheet … I think it will help popularizing the game …"[25]

Louis Little, Columbia University, "Your scoring sheet is good, but I am afraid that people would not take the time to fill it out …"[26]

George Biggers, *The Atlanta Journal* Business Manager, "Your booklet is a splendid piece of work."[27]

Stuart Stephenson, The Montgomery Advertiser … "Splendid scoring sheet. I congratulate you on your vision …"[28]

Grantland Rice, "Looked over your scoring sheet. I find no detail that you overlooked."[29]

Louis Little, Columbia University, NYC: "I would be more than happy to help you in any way I can if you feel that showing my letter would be of assistance, go ahead and do it."[30]

Charles Bachman, Michigan State football coach: "Scoring system good; might not interest everyone. However, if I could be of help …"[31]

Jack Meagher, Alabama Polytechnic Institution, Auburn, Alabama: "Studied your chart, fine contribution."[32]

These letters were mailed to Newman between the end of 1934 through 1935. All letters were hopeful in spirit; some respondents offered opinions about who would benefit the most from the chart – the public and/or the coaching staff; some advised that it was too late in the season to attract advertisers. In the end this project was not successful, nor was his Grid Fun game, but in no way did this interfere with Zipp's future, successful projects.

Forms for Broadcasting

The venerable Grantland Rice, responding to an inquiry from Newman who suggested two forms of broadcasting, wrote on November 9, 1934, "Right now I am afraid it would be a little late for this season to get any advertiser ..." He suggested next season as better and offered to help in any way. Rice offered advice to Zipp, on whatever the matter was, down the road.

There had been discussion about Rice going into radio broadcasting. Rice, the editor of *The American Golfer* at the time, had only words of restrained encouragement for Zipp, but of what, we do not know.

His final paragraph was about what he loved. Rice said that he was attending the Tulane-Colgate game the next day. And in a reversal Rice asked Newman for advice: "I would appreciate any dope you could give me about the Alabama team. I would like to help in any way I can down that way as it looks as if Alabama might be one of the best teams."[33]

Rose Bowl Game 1935

The 1934 college football season ended with Stanford University and the University of Alabama meeting in the Rose Bowl on January 1, 1935. Both teams had achieved undefeated records except for Stanford's 7-7 tie with the Santa Clara Bulldogs, a team that represented Santa Clara University.

Dwight Pelkin, a fifteen-year old from Green Bay, Wisconsin wrote on January 3, 1935, to Zipp "Mueller" [sic] saying he listened to the Rose Bowl game and would appreciate receiving a "Southern" write-up of the game.[34] Pelkin wrote that while listening to the game on the radio he heard Zipp's name mentioned as "outstanding of the southern sportswriters." It is interesting that a fifteen-year old in "the North" would pick up on the subtle geographical distinction invading sports reporting. Indeed, the game was between California's Stanford University and the University of Alabama, Alabama winning 29-13.

The young sports fan wanted to read what Zipp thought about Dixie Howell, Bill Lee, and Don Hutson. He admitted that Alabama exceeded his expectations by such a convincing victory. And there was no way of knowing that Don Hutson would become the best Green Bay Packer of his era. Or maybe he did know, from reading newspaper reports of the Packers' scouting of college players.

The 1930s

Pelkin asked Zipp for the price of the edition of the newspaper covering the game and the price of sending the paper to him. "I am sorry I haven't got the money at present for a 3-cent stamped self-addressed envelope [sic] but I'll make it up to you in my return letter."

1935 Orange Bowl, Sugar Bowl, Rose Bowl

The State of Florida and the City of Miami were both flat broke. For the first Orange Bowl football game, it was the Bowl planners' intention to pit a northern school against a southern school to bring in northern money.[35]

The first Sugar Bowl game was played in New Orleans. Fred Digby and Zipp Newman had talked about a Sugar Bowl for years. Tulane defeated Temple 20-14 in the inaugural.[36] On the west coast the Rose Bowl was celebrating its twenty-first renewal.

Broadcasting

Grantland Rice, in a second letter to Zipp in February 12, 1935, wrote: "I don't know what my plans are yet in regard to radio ..."[37] Apparently, Newman had petitioned Rice about the possibility of Rice entering the broadcasting booth for one of the national radio networks. Nothing came of it.

Ford Motor Company

Ford Motor Company's General Sales Manager [the signature indecipherable] wrote to Zipp on March 4, 1935, saying that "Mr. Jerome "Dizzy" Dean has written Mr. Ford on your behalf regarding a sports feature to be added to our broadcasting feature of the World Series ... we do not believe we would be interested in any football score features as there is not one big game which arouses universal attention; this is a sectional proposition."[38]

It is interesting that Dizzy Dean wrote to Ford Motor Company on Zipp's behalf. It is not known when Zipp and Dean met, but it is likely that the Dixie Series games between Houston and Birmingham could have been the occasion of their first meeting. Regardless, Zipp, as a good reporter, would let no opportunity go by without interviewing any star player, particularly knowing how Zipp's Birmingham readers loved baseball.

Jesse Owens, Alabama native, won the 100-meter race at the Berlin Olympics on August 3, 1936.[39]

Zipp the Advocate

No one today would remember baseball pitcher Phil Douglas. But many people would recognize the name, or at least had heard stories of Judge Kenesaw Mountain Landis. Landis was the first Major League Baseball Commissioner. The baseball club owners selected Landis for cleaning up their game following the scandal in the World Series of 1919 of the Chicago White Sox, dubbed "Black Sox." Landis ruled Organized Baseball with an iron fist.

There was a minor league pitcher, originally a catcher, who threw out twelve players in a single game. That got the attention of the majors. Phil Douglas played in the majors off and on, off and on because he was a heavy drinker. He played for several teams but when playing for the New York Giants he ran into trouble with the team's manager who was, at first, trying to assist Douglas with his drinking problems. But in the short and long terms that assistance failed. The two men hated one another.

Douglas was fed up with the team's manager and wanted to get back at him. He penned a letter to baseball player Les Mann requesting help. Mann was neither a drinker nor smoker, a religious person of high character. Mann was shocked by what he read in the letter from Douglas.

The Giants were on the verge of winning the National League Pennant and Douglas knew that he was key to winning. But the Giants' manager, John McGraw, treated Douglas in a manner that would have landed McGraw in jail today. In his August 7, 1922 letter Douglas said he wanted an inducement to make sure McGraw did not win the pennant. He asked Mann to "send a man over here with the goods, and I will leave home on the next train" thereby leaving the Giants without their star pitcher.

Mann gave the letter to his manager, Branch Rickey. After a time of thinking through the contents of the letter, Rickey notified Commissioner Landis.

Eventually there was a meeting with Landis, Douglas, and McGraw, and others. The key question Landis asked Douglas was "Did you write the letter?" Yes. That was the end of Phil Douglas's baseball career. His life was even more miserable from that time forward. He played for several independent and semi-pro teams, including a team in Birmingham, Alabama. But as he aged his baseball skills diminished and he was driving trucks and worked in a factory manufacturing, of all things, baseballs.

In 1936, now age 46, Douglas wrote to Zipp Newman asking for his assistance in getting re-instated into Organized Baseball.

> "I think I have been treated unfair [sic] but I have not the means to fight it. It has worked many hardships and caused me many heartaches, thing hanging over my good name. I love baseball and as you know was always in there for a lot of games every year. I surely need help, and any other information I can give I'll be glad to do so. Nothing would do me more good than to have a chance to come back to life." [40]

It is not known whether Newman and Douglas had much contact during the course of any baseball season, major or minor. But Newman wrote to Commissioner Landis saying that he thought "Phil was weak, never bad." Commissioner Landis rejected Zipp's request for Douglas's re-instatement; however, Landis sent Douglas a personal check to help him get by. Another plea made in 1990 was also rejected.

Cedartown, Georgia native Phil Douglas, died in Sequatchie County, Tennessee on August 1, 1952. He was sixty-two.

Woodward sells Barons and Rickwood

On February 7, 1938 A.H. Woodward sold both the Birmingham Barons baseball team and Rickwood Field. Businessman Ed Norton paid $175,000. Woodward's company went bankrupt and needed the cash. [41]

Newman Model Home Open House

Zipp Newman opens his model home to the public for the last time. A Sears-Roebuck sponsored home on Montevallo Road in Mountain Brook Estates had been open for three weeks when a newspaper article, complete with pictures, warned Mr. and Mrs. Birmingham that today, Sunday, October 16, 1938, is the last day that they "will have an opportunity to see the model home on Montevallo Road ..." The house was a white brick bungalow and touted as being the only fire-proof home in all of Birmingham. More than 15,000 people visited the home leading up to this day. [42]

Frances Newman Morris

Monday Morning Quarterback Club

By 1939 sports was integral to southern culture and Birmingham appeared to be its natural center. Geographically centered relative to the other states of the South, Alabama – and Birmingham, its largest city – became the "capital" of southern sports. The emergence of this sports leadership was due in no small part to the actions and sportswriting of Zipp Newman. It seemed logical that Newman and other sports enthusiasts create and establish the Monday Morning Quarterback Club.[43]

The future would see an expansion or birthing of other sports and non-sporting events that would change the face of Birmingham for the better against a negative society background. The MMQBC would become the platform for charitable work, most notable the Crippled Children's Clinic Football Game.

Crippled Children's Clinic Football Game

The first Crippled Children's Clinic Football Game in Birmingham, played on December 14, 1935, was a brainchild of Zipp Newman or at least a shared vision with his friend, Dr. John D. Sherrill.[44] This game was a flop in terms of net receipts. It garnered little more than seven hundred dollars to forward to the Clinic. The planning of the game was well-supported with the advice of Alabama head coach Frank Thomas and Auburn head coach Jack Meagher. Something needed to change.

The athletes who played in the games between the years 1935 and 1938 were contributed by the Freshman football team at Birmingham-Southern College. But Birmingham-Southern gave up football in 1938. No game was played in 1939. Trustees for the Clinic approached Zipp Newman to plan and arrange a game for 1940. Freshmen teams from Auburn University and Howard College [now Samford University) played in 1940 and 1941. Then Howard decided to shut down its football program. World War II now had its grip on America and its institutions and in 1942 Mississippi State played Auburn.

But it was in 1943 that George Mattison, Homer Thomas, and Zipp Newman came up with a new plan for the Clinic charity game. From this point forward, the game was to be played on Thanksgiving Day at Birmingham's Legion Field between two top football teams from Birmingham high schools. This arrangement turned out to be workable and successful as a fund-raising event for the Clinic, and Zipp Newman has since then been credited as the main person responsible for its success.[45]

It was clear to any observer that Newman not only possessed great promotional skills, probably from hundreds of well-written articles honed over the years, but held a high degree of organizational skill. Wrapped with the tact of persuasion – or arm-twisting finesse – Newman was the person other leaders called upon to get things done, successfully. The "ole Duster" or the "Boss" or just Zipp, was the main man.

---

[1] 1930 United States Census, Birmingham, Jefferson County, Alabama, Precinct 37, enumerated on April 23, 1930.

[2] Barra, 93, taken from Robert Gregory's book, 69.

[3] Barra, 98-99; *The Birmingham News*, 9-15-1931

[4] Black, Art [and other books]

[5] Barra, 103; *The Birmingham News*, 9-15-1931

[6] Barra, 105; *The Birmingham News*, 9-24-1931

[7] http://www.secsports.com/article/12628010/sec-history

[8] A.B. "Happy" Chandler letter to Zipp on Inter-Southern Life Insurance Company letterhead on 12-19-1932

[9] Timothy Whitt, *Bases Loaded with History: the Story of Rickwood Field, America's Oldest Baseball Park* (Birmingham, Ala.: R. Boozer Press, 1995), 85.

[10] A.H. Woodward, Woodward Iron Company letterhead, January 29, 1934

[11] W.A. Alexander, Georgia Tech Athletic Association letterhead, November 9, 1934

[12] Joseph Bihler, The Christy Walsh Syndicate letterhead, November 22, 1934

[13] O.B. Keeler, *Atlanta Journal* letterhead, November 21, 1934

[14] Dan E. McGugin, Vanderbilt University Athletic Association, November 15, 1934.

[15] H.D. Drew, The University of Alabama Athletic Association letterhead, February 2, 1935

[16] C.A. Wynne letter on University of Kentucky letterhead, February 7, 1935.

[17] P.B. Parker, University of Tennessee letterhead, February 7, 1935.

[18] Frank Thomas, University of Alabama Athletic Association letterhead, February 7, 1935

[19] Henry Mehre, University of Georgia – Department of Athletics letterhead, February 7, 1935

[20] Wallace Wade, Duke University letterhead, February 9, 1935

[21] Bernie Bierman, University of Minnesota letterhead, February 11, 1935

[22] NBC San Francisco, National Broadcasting Company letterhead, February 12, 1935

[23] E.P. Madigan, St. Mary's College-California letterhead, February 12, 1935

[24] Edmond Armes, The Travelers Insurance Co. letterhead, Birmingham, February 15, 1935

[25] Ted Cox, Tulane Athletic Council letterhead, New Orleans, February 18, 1935

[26] Louis Little, Columbia University letterhead, New York City, February 19, 1935

[27] George Biggers, The Atlanta Journal letterhead, Atlanta, February 21, 1935

[28] Stuart Stephenson, The Montgomery Advertiser, Montgomery, February 25, 1935

[29] Grantland Rice, The American Golfer letterhead, New York City, February 27, 1935

[30] Louis Little, Columbia University letterhead, March 4, 1935

[31] Charles Bachman, Michigan State College letterhead, East Lancing, Michigan, March 5, 1935

[32] Jack Meagher, Alabama Polytechnic Institute, Auburn, Alabama, March 6, 1935

[33] Grantland Rice, The American Golfer letterhead, November 9, 1934

[34] Dwight Pelkin, handwritten letter, January 3, 1935

[35] Newman, Zipp. *The Impact of Southern Football*. (Montgomery: Morris-Bell Publishing Company, 1969), 85.

[36] Newman, Zipp. *The Impact of Southern Football.* (Montgomery: Morris-Bell Publishing Company, 1969), 71-72.

[37] Grantland Rice, The American Golfer letterhead, New York City, February 27, 1935

[38] Ford Motor Company, Dearborn, Michigan, March 4, 1935

[39] https://en.wikipedia.org/wiki/Jesse_Owens

[40] David Pietrusza, *Judge and Jury: the Life and Times of Judge Kenesaw Mountain Landis* (South Bend, Ind.: Diamond Communications, 1998), 253, 254.

[41] Timothy Whitt, *Bases Loaded with History: The Story of Rickwood Field, America's Oldest Baseball Park* (Birmingham, Ala.: R. Boozer Press, 1995), 59.

[42] "Zipp Newman's Residence Will Be Open to Public Last Time Sunday." *The Birmingham News*, October 16, 1938.

[43] https://www.mmqbc.org/about-us/

[44] Alabama High School Football Historical Society:
http://www.ahsfhs.org/articles2014/1935allstargame.asp

[45] Monday Morning Quarterback Club program for the "23rd Annual Football Dinner," December 14, 1961.

1940s

Introduction

The population of Birmingham stagnated between 1930 and the beginning of the 1940s. It grew only 0.1 % to 267,583. However, it was still Alabama's lead city in many respects. Zipp Newman's achievements seemed to have reached their best during the 1940s.

By the time of the U.S Census enumeration on April 20, 1940, Zipp and Mary Frances had a family. Now with two daughters, Meredith,7, and Frances, 5, the family lived in the Sears-Roebuck model home at 2959 Montevallo Road in the Jefferson County subdivision of Mountain Brook Estates.[1]

The world had been at war since 1939 and the United States had not entered the fighting in early 1941. But approximately 130 miles south-southeast of Birmingham at Tuskegee Institute, training began on April 24, 1941 of African-American military pilots. [2] On Monday, December 8, 1941, President Franklin D. Roosevelt addressed Congress, asking for a declaration of war with the Empire of Japan. The United States government and its industries geared up for wartime production of vital services for the military. The security of the nation was primary. Americans at home carried on with their lives, as usual.

Organizational Leadership

Fred Digby, the general manager of the Sugar Bowl and a former sports editor of *The New Orleans Item*, was succeeded as president of the Southern Football Writers Association by Newman. Zipp was also named president of the newly-formed National Federation of Baseball Writers Association. The minor leagues in baseball, which were many in the 1940s, elected Newman president at their annual meeting in Atlanta. Vice presidents were chosen to oversee AA, A1, and A leagues.

The Birmingham News and *The Age-Herald* did much to promote their sports columnists. In the promotional "Greatest Galaxy of Star

Football Writers In History of These Newspapers Are Ready for the Season to Begin – Local Writers Who Will Cover the Entire South," seven sportswriters were pictured with descriptors of their contributions to readers. They were: Price Howard, Jimmy Roberts, Jack House, Bob Phillips, Jerry Bryan, Henry Vance, and Zipp Newman.

The promotion, for example, stated that Henry "Hy" Vance

> "is in training to bring readers of *The Birmingham News-Age Herald* his greatest assortment of similes, humor and crow pictures. Every sport has its great humorist. Vance is the King of all football humorists. He presents a football game in a style of his own."

Newman, the article promoted,

> "has been covering football games for this newspaper for 21 years. That makes him the dean of football writers of the South. Nobody knows more football than Mr. Newman – nobody knows better how to write impressions of the game, telling just what happened and how it happened to happen. He has written as an eyewitness of all the intersectional clashes for years and probably knows more stars, more ex-stars, more coaches and more ex-coaches than any sports writer south of the Mason-Dixon line. Follow Zipp and be ahead of the rest of the field on happenings on the gridiron."

Vance and Newman collaborated on many sporting projects through the years they both worked. Vance had for a time veered from his sportswriting and dabbled in writing fiction. He had several of his stories published in magazines. In 1942 the two sportswriters jointly penned "The Sacrifice Hit" which was published in the July 1942 issue of *Esquire* magazine.[3] The story was about turkey hunting. "Both [men] are chicken-eating turkey hunters, but all right guys just the same."[4]

The first Birmingham Negro High School Football Game to fight tuberculosis was played in 1943. This game, too, was Newman-inspired and MMQBC supported. The East-West high school football game for Alabama Sight Conservation Corps was played the following year. Another Newman innovation.

Zipp Newman Day #1

The Birmingham Kiwanis Club celebrated what turned out to be the first "Zipp Newman Day" on February 20, 1945, at a luncheon in the *Tutwiler Hotel* in downtown Birmingham. The well-attended event was headlined by guest speaker Grantland Rice. Two other speakers honoring Newman were George A. Mattison, Jr., Chairman of the Crippled Children's Clinic Football Game and member of the Board of Directors of the Clinic; and Ed Norton, member of the MMQBC and the Kiwanis Club.[5] Norton was at one time owner of the Birmingham Barons baseball club, having purchased the club from Rick Woodward.

George Mattison, Jr. was a wealthy Birmingham industrialist.[6] Four years Zipp's junior, the two men worked well together, particularly in the organization of the Monday Morning Quarterback Club. Both men were pro-Birmingham and worked to bring growth to the area. Mattison is responsible for bringing in several businesses to Birmingham and Newman made Birmingham a sports journalism centerpiece. Together they worked to bring about the expansion of the Crippled Children's Clinic. Grantland Rice is a name that many Americans recognize. Like Zipp, Rice's career began in sportswriting. Rice is famous for giving the title of the *Four Horsemen* to the backfield of the University of Notre Dame's football team. A learned man in sports, his career made him a sports authority.[7] Given the exchange of letters between Rice and Newman and their shared love of sports, it was fitting that on this *Zipp Newman Day* Grantland Rice would deliver the main address. It was a high honor.

President Franklin Delano Roosevelt died in Georgia on April 12, 1945.

CCC Football Game 1945

On Thanksgiving Day 1945 the ninth Crippled Children's Clinic Football Game was played between Ensley and West End, two of the five high schools in Birmingham, Alabama. In the game's program, director of athletics Homer L. Thomas wrote that "This is not an exhibition game." The two teams were tied for first place in Alabama high school competition, and this game would count.[8]

The game program reminded attendees that the Crippled Children's Clinic games were the state's largest drawing card and "one of the most colorful sporting events in the South."

The Birmingham News company took over sponsorship of the game in 1940 and began paying the event's expenses, insuring a larger payout for the Clinic. It was noted that the idea for sponsoring the event was the result of a meeting between Dr. John D. Sherrill and Zipp Newman while in Lexington, Kentucky at a football game. Sherrill was at that time the surgical director of the Clinic and had the idea for a sponsorship of an annual game to raise money for operating expenses. The first game was in 1936.

The program's cover pictured the architect's drawing of the proposed new home of the Clinic. An inside page pictured Zipp Newman and George Mattison. It cited Newman for his vision, initiative and energy; and Mattison for his energy and interest in the Clinic as a great factor in promoting public interest. Also pictured on the same page were supporters of the clinic: Mrs. William J. Cabaniss;[9] J.M.G. Parker; Mrs. Frank P. Samford; L.M. Bargeron; C.W. (Bill) Street [sic], Jr.; and John W. Black.

Alabama beat Southern California 34-14 in the 1946 Rose Bowl game.[10] This was the last time that the University of Alabama played in a Rose Bowl game. Of its six appearances, Alabama's record is 4-1-1. Zipp Newman attended and reported on all six Alabama appearances. He also traveled with the Georgia Tech team to the 1929 Rose Bowl Game. Georgia Tech defeated California 8-7.

Bill Cunningham wrote in *The Birmingham News*, on January 26, 1946, an article headlined, "Heart of Dixie Beats for Kids: Sports Editor's Idea Grows Into Children's Hospital." Writing about the work leading to the planned new hospital, Cunningham said,

> "There's probably not another story such as this one in the history of sport. It began in the usual fashion as a weekly luncheon of football filberts met to rag the coaches and officials and have a lot of fun. And, as in that other great and highly successful southern civic project, the New Orleans Sugar Bowl, the idea here came from another quiet but widely respected and loved local sports editor – in this case, Zip [sic] Newman."

Cunningham was referring to Birmingham's Monday Morning Quarterback Club which, as an organization, dedicated its efforts three years earlier to the building and equipping of a clinic for crippled children.[11] Newman's personal dedication to this long-term project and its relationship to the MMQBC, speaks to the earlier formation of Civitan International and its change of purpose from a self-centered organization to a service organization.

Newman was not just a supporter of major and minor league sports; he involved himself with other organizations such as the Shades Valley "Y." At its annual meeting on April 12, 1946, Zipp introduced University of Alabama football coach Frank Thomas to the three hundred fifty persons in attendance. Granted, either Thomas or Newman would have drawn a large group of admirers. On this Friday evening the vice chairman of this "Y" acted as master of ceremonies. With him were Chairman of the "Y" Jack Allison and Lynn Strickland, a director of the "Y."[12]

Kentucky Derby 1946

Sportswriters have fun. The seventy-second running of the Kentucky Derby on Saturday May 4, 1946, attracted fifty-five sportswriters from across the nation, including Grantland Rice and Zipp Newman. *The Birmingham News* published in its Friday edition the predictions of the fifty-five sportswriters for "win, place, and show." The favorite going into the race was the leader of the three-horse entry of Mrs. Elizabeth Graham, Lord Boswell. Twenty-one of the sportswriters wrote that Lord Boswell would win.

Zipp predicted Knockdown, Perfect Bahram, and Lord Boswell for his win, place, and show. Grantland Rice selected Marine Victory, Hampden, and Spy Song. The race ended with Assault winning, then Spy Song and Hampden.[13] Two writers, Bob Considine of the International News Service and Robert Kelly of the New York Racing Association, picked Assault to win.[14]

In 1947 the University of Pittsburgh recruited Dr. Jonas Salk. He worked for three years at Pittsburgh in search of a cure for polio. There was a national effort to eliminate this disease. Zipp had been working on caring for children with the disease for years. At one time there were 15,000 cases of polio in Alabama.

The Dixie Bowl, Birmingham, and SEC Policy

"In 1947, after World War II, in Gainesville, Florida, the Southeastern Conference outlawed all bowl games. Bill Alexander moved to hold the vote until after lunch. During lunch, Bill got into a selling job, and the afternoon saw an affirmative vote to participate in only the Sugar Bowl, Rose Bowl, and Orange Bowl. It killed the blooming Dixie Bowl in Birmingham."[15] Zipp was advisor to the organizers, not only to the Sugar and Orange Bowl organizers, but the Dixie Bowl also. That decision concerning the Dixie Bowl, though negatively impacting Birmingham, would be placed in the back rows of history in 1948.

The Walls

For Henry Hardin "Zipp" Newman, the 1930s represented a decade of hard work and a dedication to sports reporting and helping people in need. The 1940s saw, among the many activities of Newman, the precursor of a sports hall of fame.

An article in *The Birmingham News* headlined "For The Sports-Minded" provided a brief and robust description of a large room in the newspaper's new office building with walls of pictures of the greatest figures of that era. The walls were carefully arranged in panels depicting the history of sports in America from its beginnings to the current day. Indeed, the staff of the sports department sat approvingly of the visually delightful display.

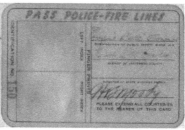

The thinking behind the walls' development was, according to the article, the "Happy Sovereign, 'Newman the Zipper,'" the possessor of an encyclopedic knowledge of sports. The collection was quite unique and so precious that the Rector of the Episcopal Church of the Advent, in downtown Birmingham, John Turner, dedicated the vast room with words of benediction.

Every recognized sport was represented on those walls: football, baseball, track sports, rowing, swimming, hunting, fishing, horse racing, boxing and wrestling. The writer of the article said the office is open every day of the week and that the "experience will educate you." The future Alabama Sports Hall of Fame was represented in this office archive.[16] In 1947 the walls were dedicated as *The Birmingham News-Age-Herald* Sports Galleries.

The North Wall captured the
                  1935 Rose Bowl Champs Coaches
                  The Sport of Kings
                  Women Sports Champions

The East Wall depicted the
                  Cream of Track and Field
                  Baseball Hall of Fame
                  Famous Coaches and Stadia

The South Wall displayed the
                  Early Indianapolis Speedway
                  Churchill Downs
                  Helms Athletic Foundation Citation
                  Four Famous Golfers
                  Baron Pennant Winners
                  Grantland Rice
                  Judge Kenesaw Mountain Landis
                  Dan McGugin
                  Michael "Mike" Donahue
                  George A. Mattison, Jr.

The West Wall, for example, provided memories of
                  All-Time Football Teams of Alabama and Auburn
                  The All-America Board of Football
                  Amos Alonzo Stagg
                  Wallace Wade
                  Mel Allen
                  The Football Paterson Family

The four walls represented a fine and unique collection. According to its dedication pamphlet, the photos were assembled from England, France, Italy, Germany, Australia, Scotland, Canada and the United States. The Galleries featured celebrities from all fields of sports, famed tennis courts, golf courses, baseball parks, football stadia and race tracks of the world. And there was a Room of Color which contained some of the most beautiful wildlife and sports color prints assembled in any one collection.[17]

Sports, however, was only one side of Zipp Newman's "people coin." The flip side of his coin was his concern for people who needed help, particularly children living with polio. Newman began working this side of the coin in the previous decade. But the 1940s was the decade of recognition.

Show Biz and the Clinic

On August 7, 1947, Georgiana, Alabama native, Hank Williams, signed his first recording contract with MGM to become a regular performer on the radio show *Louisiana Hayride*.[18] Elvis Presley would make his first appearance on the show six years later. But it was Mary "Bebe" Anderson, an actress and Birmingham native, who planned and held the premiere of her starring role movie, "Whispering City" at Birmingham's Empire Theatre on November 20, 1947. It was no accident that this movie opening coincided with the playing of the Crippled Children's Game. The proceeds from the movie opening benefitted the Children's Clinic.

SEC Headquarters Moves to Birmingham

Bernie Moore became the second full-time Commissioner of the Southeastern Conference on Feb. 21, 1948, when the office was moved to Birmingham. Moore, a former LSU coach, guided the SEC to national respect in his eighteen-year tenure.[19] In Zipp's book *The Impact of Southern Football*, Moore wrote in the *Foreword* that the SEC office was near *The Birmingham News* and that he and Newman saw each other almost daily for eighteen years.[20]

Alf Van Hoose wrote that the reason the Southeastern Conference headquarters moved to Birmingham was because of Zipp.

Penchant for Statistics Continued

Walt Dropo hit the longest home run at Rickwood Field on May 21, 1948. Alf Van Hoose estimated the hit at 486 feet. Bob Scranton said it was Zipp who called and wanted to get a picture of Dropo standing close to where the ball was hit. A plaque was placed there. The Birmingham Barons' general manager, Eddie Glennon, never understood the homerun's value.[21]

The Honors

Cooper Green was, more or less, the mayor of the City of Birmingham in 1948. The structure of city government at that time was that of a three-person commission. Green's official title was President of the Commission of the City of Birmingham.

On September 13, 1948, Mayor Green issued a proclamation designating September 15, 1948, a Wednesday, as "Zip [sic] Newman Day." The proclamation read, in part:

> "WHEREAS, Zipp Newman, sports editor of the Birmingham News,
> has received the high honor of being selected by the American
> Hospital Association as one of the fifty persons in the United States
> who have done the most for American Hospitals ..."[22]

The Proclamation further acknowledged that Zipp Newman had harnessed sports for health, particularly in the annual high school baseball and football sporting events.

The mayor also noted in his Proclamation that since the Birmingham Lions Club was celebrating Newman and his accomplishments as "Zipp Newman Day" on September 15, he thought it appropriate to designate that day for the entire city.

American Hospital Association Honors Newman

Ten days following the twenty-second Miss America Pageant in Atlantic City, New Jersey, and within one week when Newman was honored by his local Lions Club and the City of Birmingham, the American Hospital Association held its fiftieth anniversary convention in the Claridge Hotel, one of Atlantic City's finest. The main address at their awards ceremony was delivered by the Honorable Lister Hill, United States Senator from Alabama. It was at this ceremony that the non-medical professional Henry Hardin Newman was made an Honorary Member of the Association.

Arthur L. Bailey, administrator of the Jefferson-Hillman Hospital in Birmingham, was the person who nominated Zipp for the honor. Bailey's letter of nomination included the following:

"Zipp's contribution did not come through wealth, of which he has little, it came through fine leadership and spirit. It came through a leadership and spirit that has guided this whole community to do outstanding work for sick people who can't pay for their own care."[23]

The citation dated September 21, 1948, honored Newman for his many efforts on behalf of others. The citation in part stated:

"Combining your position in the sports world with your conviction that every person has a right to health regardless of his means, you have demonstrated yourself to be a leading citizen of Alabama and of the nation in developing hospital and medical care." [24]

One week after the Atlantic City convention, Zipp received a letter from the hospital association's Executive Director, George Bugbee.

"Hospital administrators and trustees from over the continent have told me how much they were impressed that evening, how they enjoyed meeting you or wished they could have done so ... We are proud to have you now as an Honorary Member of the Association ..."[25]

Birmingham celebrated even more.

Newman and his wife Frances were pictured in the Birmingham newspapers receiving the certificate awarded to Zipp by the American Hospital Association. The pictures included Senator Lister Hill and Mr. Graham Davis, the retiring president of the association.

After the picture-taking session, Mrs. Newman traveled to New York to visit with friends. Zipp, ever the sports enthusiast and journalist, returned to Birmingham but from there he went to New Orleans to view and report on the Alabama-Tulane football game. Played on Saturday, September 24, 1948, the University of Alabama lost 14-21, a game attended by 65,000 spectators. Alabama's season was a poor 4-4-1. Tulane University ended their season with a 9-1 record, losing only to Georgia Tech.[26]

Newsweek magazine published an article about Zipp Newman on December 6, 1948. The magazine lauded the lifetime efforts of Newman for his work for the Crippled Children's Clinic and its funding through sporting events. The article could not have been more flattering. It opened with:

> "Sports-loving Southerners look up to sports writers with the same awed respect with which Broadway regards Winchell or Hollywood a Hedda Hopper. So Alabamians simply take it for granted that, come Thanksgiving, they'll turn out for 'ol Zipp's game."

Newsweek also said that Zipp, though soft-spoken, could roll off rules and records from an elephant-like memory.[27]

Zipp Newman Day #2

Civitan International, an organization founded in Birmingham, honored Newman on Friday, May 13, 1949. During that week from May 9 to May 15, the organization observed nationally what they termed "Good Citizenship Observance Week." Throughout the nation local Civitan clubs honored citizens who, in their judgement, made outstanding contributions to their communities. The ideal tagged to the honor was "Builder of Good Citizenship." Zipp Newman was the person selected by the Civitan Club for 1949.

Civitan noted that Zipp "is a national celebrity due to his unusual and outstanding stature as a sports writer and in this city is known and loved as a four-square citizen," a trait designating a solid and dependable

The 1940s

person. Citing Zipp's fund-raising events over the years, the Civitan Club acknowledged that,

> "Through this [fund-raising] project, several hundred thousand dollars have been raised to finance a new hospital for unfortunate crippled children. This [hospital] structure will soon be erected at the University of Alabama Medical Center."

Four persons gave speeches honoring Newman: Robert Strong, President of the Crippled Children's Clinic; James Downey, President of the Amateur Baseball Association; The Reverend John Turner, Rector of the Episcopal Church of the Advent-Birmingham; and Harry Bradley, the Business Manager of *The Birmingham News*.[28]

Robert Strong said that Zipp was the inspiration that brought about realization of the hospital through funds raised between champion high school teams. He also told the Civitan Club that a chapel in the new hospital will be dedicated to Mr. Newman.

Zipp's boss, Harry Bradley, said that he thought Zipp had been torn for years between his love for sports and newspapering and his interest in hospital work and "he has been able to do each job apparently without slighting the other."

Zipp's pastor, John Turner, extending the observations made by Mr. Bradley, said that for Zipp "These activities were not extra curriculum ones, but part and parcel of his life." But the most emotional speech was given by Zipp's boyhood friend.

Jim Downey, at the end of his speech, tried to tell the listening audience about all of the great figures helped by Zipp. At this point Downey started reading a poem that began, "When our Great Maker signals Zipp from Up Above." Emotion got the better of him and he returned to his seat with a handkerchief to his eyes.[29]

Bill Stern of NBC sent a telegram.

> "CONGRATULATIONS ON GROUND BREAKING CEREMONY WISH I COULD BE WITH YOU. IT WILL BE IN SPIRIT. YOU'VE DONE A WONDERFUL JOB REGARDS= BILL STERN NATIONAL BROADCASTING CO="[30]

Birmingham television stations begin broadcasting in 1949: stations WAPI-TV (Alabama Polytechnic Institute letters) and WBRC-TV.

Ol' Southern Colonel

Zipp's ideas kept on coming, this time about the college football bowl games. A *Pasadena Star-News* columnist, Rube Samuelsen in his "Quiet Please" column, headlined "Zipp Swings from the Floor." Opening with:

> "SAY, THAT OL' SOUTHERN COLONEL, ZIPP NEWMAN, certainly spoke his piece, didn't he? Did some good swinging, too, as well as pounding the table (and typewriter) while shouting 'South Burns Over Bowl Segregation' ..."

Zipp wanted Pacific Coast football teams and Big Ten teams to rotate bowl games at the end of the college football seasons. Newman assisted in the development of both the Sugar Bowl in New Orleans and the Orange Bowl in Miami and he did not like the idea of conferences committing just to one bowl, as the Rose Bowl game arrangement had been set up. Samuelsen mused that if the Rose Bowl did not have the commitments of the Pacific Coast and Big Ten conferences it would be left out in the cold, instead of the Orange and Sugar.[31]

It should be noted, for the record, that two years after this article was published by Samuelsen, Henry Hardin "Zipp" Newman became a "colonel."

> "To All to Whom These Presents Shall Come, Greeting: Know Ye that Honorable Zipt [sic] Newman, Birmingham, Alabama, Having Been

Duly Appointed Is Hereby Commissioned as an Aide-de-Camp on the Staff of the Governor with the Rank and Grade of Colonel. Lawrence W. Wetherby, Governor, in the one hundred and 59th Year of the Commonwealth of Kentucky, January 29, 1951."

Newman was indeed destined to become a "southern colonel."

Authorization Certificate   Colonel Newman

---

[1] United States Census 1940, Jefferson County, Birmingham, Alabama. Source: FamilySearch.org

[2] Alabama Department of Archives and History

[3] Marguerite Johnston. "About Birmingham." *The Birmingham News*. Date unknown, 1942. Their fictional story is in *Esquire*, Volume 18, July 1942, beginning on page 59.

[4] Bob Luckie. "About Birmingham." *The Birmingham News*. Day unknown, 1942.

[5] Birmingham Kiwanis Club. Program for "Zipp Newman Day," Tutwiler Hotel, Birmingham, Alabama, February 20, 1945.

[6] Alabama Academy of Honor and Alabama Department of Archives and History. http://www.archives.alabama.gov/famous/academy/g_mattis.html

[7] Britannica Online. https://www.britannica.com/biography/Grantland-Rice

[8] The Crippled Children's Clinic Football Game program, Thanksgiving Day 1945.

[9] Cabaniss was the mother of William Jelks Cabaniss, Jr. who served in the Alabama House and Senate between 1972 and 1990; was a candidate for the United States Senate; and was United States Ambassador to the Czech Republic – 2004-2006. William J. Cabaniss, Jr. and Frances "Bee" Newman Morris grew up together in Mountain Brook, Alabama.

[10] Zipp Newman. *The Impact of Southern Football*. (Montgomery: Morris-Bell Publishing Company, 1969), 35.

[11] Bill Cunningham. "Heart of Dixie Beats for Kids." *The Birmingham News*, January 26, 1946.

[12] "At Valley "Y" Meeting. *The Shades Valley Sun*, April 12, 1946.

[13] Horse Racing Nation – 1946 Kentucky Derby. https://www.horseracingnation.com/race/1946_Kentucky_Derby#

[14] "Scribes Pick Lord Boswell ro Win 72nd Kentucky Derby." *The Birmingham News*, May 3, 1946.

[15] Zipp Newman. T*he Impact of Southern Football*. 5.

[16] *The Birmingham News-Age-Herald*. Sports Galleries, June 20, 1947.

[17] *The Birmingham News-Age-Herald* Sports Galleries dedication program. June 20, 1947.

[18] Alabama Department of Archive and History

[19] http://www.secsports.com/article/12628010/sec-history

[20] Newman, Zipp. *The Impact of Southern Football*. (Montgomery: Morris-Bell Publishing Company, 1969), xvi.

[21] Allen Barra, *Rickwood Field: a Century in America's Oldest Ballpark* (New York: W.W. Norton & Company, 2010), 131fn.

[22] *Proclamation of the President of the Commission of the City of Birmingham* dated September 13, 1948 designating "Zipp Newman Day."

[23] "Hospitals Honor News Sports Chief." *The Birmingham News*, August,1948.

[24] American Hospital Association. Program for "Honor Night" Fiftieth Anniversary Convention, Trimble Hall, Claridge Hotel, Atlantic City, New Jersey, September 21, 1948.

[25] George Bugbee letter to Zipp. American Hospital Association letterhead, Chicago, Illinois, October 4, 1948.

The 1940s

[26] "To Zipp – Your Scroll Well Earned." *The Birmingham News* photo and article. September 22, 1948.

[27] "Ol' Zipp." *Newsweek*, Vol. XXXII No. 24, page 62, December 6, 1948.

[28] "Zipp Newman Day." *The Civitanian*. Vol. 10, No. 49, 1949. Birmingham Alabama.

[29] "Newman Named Citizen of the Year." *The Birmingham News*, May 14, 1949.

[30] Bill Stern. Western Union Telegram NSA825 NS.CA580 NL PD=WUX CHICAGO ILL 28=. June 28, 1949.

[31] Rube Samuelsen. "Quiet Please – South Is Burning." *Pasadena Star-News*. Monday, November 21, 1949.

The 1940s

1950s

Introduction

Birmingham's population grew by 22% at 326,037 between 1940 and 1950 and the new *Birmingham Post-Herald* newspaper opened for business.

On May 24, 1948, the famous football head coach R.R. Neyland of the University of Tennessee-Knoxville wrote to Walter Steward of the Memphis *Commercial Appeal*. The letter was a follow-up to a telephone conversation the two had earlier. Their conversation at the time was about college football's "free substitution rule."

It is interesting to observe how passionate Neyland was about the game he loved.

> "I am completely opposed to the free substitution rule. It has hurt the game of football for the spectators ... and ... has largely negated the delirious claims of its proponents, who fondly cherished the dreams that the rule would help the small schools against the larger." [1]

Most likely Neyland was threatened by the rule and, like many other coaches, would enlist support from similar-thinking coaches and from sportswriters. The relationship among sports enthusiasts, particularly between coaches and those writers in the sports media, can be of advocacy alignment or adversarial battle.

Three years later Neyland enclosed a copy of his letter to Steward in a letter to Newman. In this letter, dated March 5, 1951, Neyland said that his letter to Steward would give Newman "some ideas on the two-platoon system." The Tennessee coach was educating Zipp, one would suspect. "Proponents of the two-platoon system say that more men get to play. This is the biggest fallacy of them all." Neyland may have stretched the operational truth a little, but hyperbole is part of the game.

We do not possess any letters from Zipp to Neyland but can imagine that an ongoing dialogue between the two men was never-ceasing. Neyland wanted advocates for his point of view and he knew the power of the written word of newspaper sportswriters. [2]

Hospital for Crippled Children

On September 1, 1951, the Hospital for Crippled Children opened and was billed as the hospital "that football built" from fund-raising by Birmingham's Monday Morning Quarterback Club (MMQBC).

John M.G. Parker, in a handwritten letter to Zipp on December 5, 1951, wrote,

> "I think of you as 'Papa' of it [the Crippled Children's Clinic]."[3]

Parker was a captain in the U.S. Army in World War I, a company commander who trained and prepared troops to fight overseas.[4] Parker also knew, as did many others, that Zipp was one of the primary, if not "the" primary, person forming the Monday Morning Quarterback Club. Parker also knew that Newman was a quiet and humble man. Zipp loved sportswriting and learned to leverage the popularity of sports by supporting worthy causes.

Ten days before Christmas 1952, J.B. Cole, Jr., President of the Jack Cole Company in Birmingham, penned a "thank you letter" to Zipp for the article which mentioned his son Thornton Cole.[5] Cole wrote,

> "I just wanted you to know how deeply I appreciate your arranging for the splendid write-up that my son Thornton received in last Sunday's *News*. It meant so much to his mother and me to see him get such fine recognition in his own hometown."

On the 1953 Varsity Football Roster for the University of Alabama, Thornton Cole was listed as an eighteen-year old, 185-pound "Frosh" Left Halfback. One of the three quarterbacks listed was nineteen-year-old sophomore Bart Starr.

The 1950s

In Dyer Straights

An article by West Coast sports journalist Braven Dyer was mailed to Zipp and dated May 16, 1954. The clip was about University of Alabama football. Alabama had been to the Rose Bowl – not to the Rose Bowl game – eight times.[6] Dyer mused over a Yuletide gimmick used mostly in taverns to trick a betting partner into believing that the University of Alabama had played in the Rose Bowl eight instead of six times.

Braven Dyer was a sports reporter for the *Los Angeles Times* for much of his career. His column "Sports Parade" was widely read. Later he wrote for the Palm Springs *Desert Sun,* writing in a cleverly-named column "Desert Dyer-y [diary]." Dyer and Newman corresponded with each other and probably met at games involving California college football teams.

In 1970 Dyer, in a letter to Zipp, expressed his desire to attend the Alabama-University of Southern California game in Alabama. He asked Zipp for help in making that trip.

Zipp's Writing Style

It was characteristic of Henry Hardin "Zipp" Newman to write approvingly of people, regardless of whether a person was connected to sports. Writing critically of an event or an action did not mean writing hatefully. There was always something to be said that was good or positive. Never self-serving, Zipp helped others. Bill Hickey was one of those persons helped.

Typed on CBS-TV NYC stationery dated June 3, 1954, Hickey wrote of his adventure in New York City. Telling Zipp that he secured for himself an apartment just one day before writing his letter, he made it "OK." Before closing his letter with a "thanks for everything," Hickey wrote that he met Mel Allen the night before and that "he sends his best to you. Seems to be a nice guy – just as you described."[7]

Callahan Eye Clinic at UAB

Zipp Newman made his first trip to New Orleans in 1916. He traveled there with a Birmingham semi-pro baseball club. Fred Digby met them at the train station. [8] Fred and Zipp stopped by the old Grunewald Hotel. The hotel was built in 1893 by a Bavarian immigrant named Louis Grunewald. It was a very popular and upscale hotel in its day, with four hundred rooms. The hotel later was renamed the Roosevelt.[9]

It was on this trip that Newman and Digby began what would become a life-long friendship. Digby was the father of the New Orleans Sugar

The 1950s

Bowl. But this was 1916 and just at the beginning of their friendship. Other members of the future Sugar Bowl's executives would come to know Zipp and to correspond with him. Zipp knew how to connect people, draw people to special causes and to extend his own friendships to others.

Thirty-eight years later, Alston Callahan, an eye surgeon in Birmingham, wrote to Digby on June 3, 1954. Callahan had been working with Zipp Newman on the development of Birmingham's Eyesight Foundation, and as part of his medical practice Callahan had been making black-and-white films on various types of eye surgeries, films that he used as teaching tools. But Callahan had a new challenge facing him later that year.

The International Congress of Ophthalmology would meet in New York City at the Waldorf-Astoria Hotel in mid-September and Callahan intended to present a color film of a special type of eyelid correction that required two surgeries. He used a football analogy to explain it to Digby.

Callahan explained the necessity for two surgeries, showing that as a running back approaches the goal with the football, he is slowed but not stopped by the first tackler, but then goes down under the impact of the second tackle. This analogy was not unaided by Zipp.

Callahan wrote Digby that Zipp Newman told him that he remembered a time when Charley Trippi of the University of Georgia required two University of North Carolina tacklers to bring him down.

With all of the preliminaries presented, Callahan said he learned from Newman that Fred Digby was in a position to produce the color film. [10] The connection among Newman, Digby, and Callahan is a result of an earlier development in which Newman played a major, if not the major, role.

Callahan and his family relocated to Birmingham after the end of World War II. He wanted to start an eye hospital, and knowing that a new medical complex as part of the University of Alabama system had been established there, Dr. Callahan decided to make the move. During the war he had worked in the United States Medical Corps as chief of a 300-bed eye facility at the Northington General Hospital in Tuscaloosa. [11]

Zipp Newman was at the forefront in getting a medical center in Birmingham. Newman's work with multiple civic organizations, his direct involvement with the Crippled Children's Clinic, and his fund-raising activities, prepared the groundwork for Dr. Callahan to make medical history.

Though his attempt at promoting his football scoring sheet was not a commercial success, the feedback received from coaches, athletic directors, and sports journalists improved Newman's skill in presentation. Given Newman's use of statistics and his sense of fair play, one can sense his orientation for structure and orderliness in his profession.[12]

"We appreciate very much the constructive manner in which you approach athletics," wrote Cliff Harper. Zipp Newman made a presentation to the Alabama High School Athletic Association in Montgomery. The association's executive secretary, Cliff Harper, wrote Zipp a thank you letter dated November 4, 1954. There is no archival copy of Zipp's presentation, but much was learned through failures.

The Beginning of the End of Polio

News of the success of clinical trials in the treatment of polio was announced by Dr. Thomas Francis in a formal press conference on April 12, 1955, in Ann Arbor, Michigan on the 10th anniversary of the death of FDR.[13] This meant not only the beginning of the end of the devasting disease, it also meant that the Birmingham's Crippled Children's Clinic would become a service of the past, or it would transition into a different kind of clinic or hospital.

The Calendar

Newman was a statistician and historian. Though his beat was sports, his scope of history was broad and deep. One method of keeping track of significant events was to maintain a calendar. In a newspaper only a minimal amount of information could fit into a small block for one day in a monthly calendar. For each day the reader gets a glimpse of history. An example of this type of recorded history is November 1950.

The 1950s

November 1, 1938 Seabiscuit outran War Admiral, winner of 1937 Triple Crown – Kentucky Derby, Preakness and Belmont – by four lengths. One of turf's greatest thrillers, yes surprises.

November 2, 1935 Buckeye Stadium, Ohio, Notre Dame roared back with 3 touchdowns in 4th quarter to beat a fine Ohio State, 18-13. Story of unsung sub reaching heights before 81,000. A grid classic.

November 3, 1929 New York. Death of John E. Madden, age 73, famous member of Old Guard of Racing. Bred 2,169 winners – 6 Kentucky Derby firsts – Plaudit, Old Rosebud, Sir Barton, Paul Jones, Zev, Flying Ebony.

November 4, 1903 San Francisco. Rudy Bob Fitzsimmons lifted world's light heavyweight crown from George Gardner. Decision – 20 rounds.

November 5 – *Famous Quote* "There is only one thing in football that is more important than winning. That is to leave the field with your opponent's respect, win or lose." – Bob Zuppke, famed Illinois Coach.

November 6, 1861 Birth of Dr. James Naismith, who invented popular game of basketball. Almonte, Ont. Winger's biggest drawing card. More than 25,000,000 players throughout world.

November 7 Color Counts – Winning football teams won't change color of jerseys [sic]. Bad luck.

November 8, 1934 Ford C. Frick, schooled in writing and broadcasting baseball, was elected the 10th president of the National League. Succeeded John A. Heydler, who served 17 years.

November 9 World's Most Glamorous Horse – Dan Patch. March 1899 – July 1916. Sire, Joe Patchem. Dan. Zelica. Won 18 straight, '01 '02. Paced mile in 1:55. Grossed owners over 2 million. Traveled 10,000 miles, showed to 600,000 in '04.

November 10   *Hash Line* – When your favorite football team is backed up on its own five-yard line. Ball carrier's heaven – End Zone.

November 11, 1868   New York. the first track and field meet ever held in the United States was at Winged Foot Club.

November 12   *Famous Quote* – "They say fish should swim thrice ... first it should swim into the sea (do you mind me?), then it should swim in butter, and at last, sirrah, it should swim in good claret. *Swift-Polite Conversation.*

November 13, 1943   After Gun – Columbus, Ohio State beat Illinois, 29-26, 12 minutes after gun. Illinois tackle off-side on last play. Called back, Ohio [State] scored on 23-yard field goal.

November 14   *Unparalleled* – Sewanee beat Texas 12-0, Texas A.&M., 10-0, Tulane, 23-0, L.S.U. 34-0 and Mississippi 12-0 in five straight days of football. Austin, Houston, New Orleans, Baton Rouge, Memphis. 60-minute men.

November 15, 1908   Chicago. Nebraska won the first Western Conference five-mile cross country championship. Comstock (Chicago) led field. 28 minutes 12 seconds.

November 16, 1947   Madison Square Garden, N.Y. Don Raleigh, New York Rangers, made 3 assists in 81 seconds against Montreal Canadiens. National Hockey League.

November 17   *Voodoo* – Black cat crossing pathway, harbinger of bad luck. Belief founded because black cats companions of witches. Five-ten player – Drives in five runs and lets in ten runs.

November 18, 1903   Mike Donahue – Yale, 1903. Donahue's Auburn football teams W-98, L-36, T-6 – 1904-1922. Unbeaten-unscored on – 1908-1914. Southern champions, 1904-08-13-14. Longest streak, W-22, T-1, L.S.U. teams W-22, L-19, T-3. Invented Line Divide.

November 19   *Famous Quote* – "If all the year were playing holidays, to sport would be as tedious as to work; But when they seldom come, they wish'd for come. *Shakespeare-King Henry IV.*

November 20, *1869*   Clear Creek, Mo. Birthplace of *Clark Griffith*, owner of Washington Senators. member of Baseball's Hall of Fame, (1891-1908). Won 237, lost 140. One of game's smartest pitchers.

November 21, *1931* – South Bend. Southern California broke National Champion Notre Dame's 25-game winning streak in story book finish, 16-14. Trojans score points in 4th period. Won on 23-yard field goal.

November 22, *1908* – Tokio, Japan. A.G. Reach's All-American team, first Major league ball players ever to visit Orient, defeated Waseda U., 18-1; Keio, 6-0 in double-header.

The 1950s

November 24, 1917   Camp Sheridan, Montgomery – Auburn's muchly under rated Tigers played Ohio State's great eleven to scoreless tie. Auburn stopped four bucks on 1-yard line. Played for service men.

November 25, 1903   Chicago. Western Conference adopted rule requiring athletes must first complete a full semester's work in residence. To prohibit roving players, more stringent scholastic requirement.

November 26, 1926   (SUNDAY) Soldier's Field. Undefeated Navy and once defeated Army battled to bone-crushing 21-all tie before 110,000. Army tied the score at 14-all in 2nd, led 21-14 at end of 3rd. Football's most famous tie game.

November 27, 1920   George Gipp, Notre Dame's all-time halfback, played his last game against Northwestern, died December 14. Walter Camp All-America, *"Win one for the Gipper."*

November 28, 1901   Hartford, Conn. *Young Corbett* won the world's featherweight championship with a knockout in second round from Terry McGovern.

November 29, 1916   St. Louis. the Women's National Bowling Association organized. Bowling is one of most popular of all sports for women, with more than 50,000 women bowling in leagues throughout the country.

November 20, 1905   Chicago. Chicago spilled Michigan in the snow, 2-0, ending Hurry Up Yost's Michigan team's string of 57 straight wins. One of the first great upsets in football.

Letters of 1959 and Zipp Retires

The 1950s letters to Zipp closed with two 1959 letters concerning "Goat" Hale. Edwin Hale played football for Mississippi College in Clinton, Mississippi. Hale played from 1915 to 1916, then served in World War I, and played again from 1920 to 1921. Hale was wounded in the War and was considered missing-in-action but was later found in France in a hospital. Hale is considered the best player at Mississippi College.[14]

There are two letters dated the same day – December 30, 1959 – in the file of Zipp Newman at the *Alabama Sports Hall of Fame* archives. Written by Robert L. Brannon, Sr., neither letter is addressed to Zipp but copied to Zipp. The first letter is addressed to "Goat"[15] citing and including a copy of another letter from Brannon to Jimmy McDowell. McDowell was Sports Editor of the *State-Times* newspaper in Jackson, Mississippi.

The second, to McDowell, in effect began the process of promoting "Goat" Hale for induction into the National Football Hall of Fame.[16] Brannon cited Clark Randolph "Dudy" Noble as a "substantiating witness" who was a coach of Hale in 1916 and an opposing coach when Noble was at Mississippi State, to Hale's athletic capabilities. Brannon went on to write that Zipp Newman had requested Noble earlier in 1959 to pick an all-time team of great football players. On Noble's list was "Goat" Hale.

To his letter to McDowell, Brannon attached a UPI newspaper clipping "'Goat' Hale Nominated for 'Hall'." Zipp's support and expertise would be used in this process for electing Hale.

Robert Brannon was the football team manager at Mississippi College when Hale was a player. At the time he wrote this letter he was living in Montgomery, Alabama and was a Commercial Agent for the Atlanta and West Point Railway of Alabama Georgia Railroad.

Edwin "Goat" Hale and his friend Jerrell "Fid" Jones operated the Hale and Jones Athletic Supplies on South Lamar Street in Jackson, Mississippi.[17]

1959 was the year that Henry Hardin "Zipp" Newman retired from *The Birmingham News*. For Newman to retire was a stretch of the imagination. He continued to write his column and took on the title of Sports Editor Emeritus.

Sporting Luminary Biographies at the Ready
In his "so-called" retirement Zipp Newman kept a ready file of sports figures from Alabama who achieved great success. He limited these bios to one typed sheet of paper. This information was always available to him when he needed to extract content for a news article. Here are a few examples of Newman's one-pagers.

LEAH MARIE RAWLS ATKINS

Zipp had a headline reading "Alabama's First World' Water Ski Champion." At age 16 Rawls won the Alabama Junior Division in Guntersville, Alabama; won First Place overall at Ontario Championships, Southampton, Canada. Both in 1951. In 1952 Rawls won the Dixie Tournament in Cypress Gardens; in 1953 Rawls won the overall National Championship in Los Angeles. Today Dr. Leah Rawls Atkins is an Alabama historian of note.

JOE LOUIS BARROW

Born in Lexington, Alabama, Louis began his boxing career in the Golden Gloves tournaments in Detroit, Michigan. He was inducted into the Army in 1942 and earned almost five million dollars.

PAUL WILLIAM BRYANT

At the time Zipp's one-pager headlined Bryant as the "Nation's Winningest Coach." He won National Champions in college football in 1961-64-65. He was voted Coach of the Year in 1961. Bryant's coaching career was documented as Maryland, Kentucky, Texas A&M, and Alabama.

Henry Hardin "Zipp" Newman continued to write in retirement but one can detect a shift in his focus, in his purpose.

---

[1] R.R. Neyland, University of Tennessee Athletic Association letterhead, Knoxville, May 24, 1948
[2] R.R. Neyland. The University of Tennessee letterhead, March 5, 1951
[3] John M.G. Parker. Handwritten letter, December 5, 1951.
[4] Catherine Pittman Smith, *Mountain Brook*, Images of America (Charleston, South Carolina: Arcadia Publishing, 2014), 28.
[5] J.B. Cole, Jr. Jack Cole Company letterhead, Birmingham, December 15, 1952

The 1950s

[6] Frances Innis. Handwritten note with article by Braven Dyer. Note is dated May 16, 1954

[7] Bill Hickey. CBS-TV, NYC letterhead, June 3, 1954.

[8] Newman. *Impact*, 71-72.

[9] http://therooseveltneworleans.com/about-the-waldorf/history/hotel-history.html

[10] Alston Callahan, MD. June 3, 1954.

[11] http://www.archives.alabama.gov/famous/academy/a_callah.html

[12] Cliff Harper. Executive Secretary, Alabama High School Athletic Association letterhead. December 4, 1954.

[13] Polio Cure announcement, April 12, 1955.

[14] https://en.wikipedia.org/wiki/Edwin_Hale

[15] Robert L. Brannon, Sr. Copy of typed letter to E.W. "Goat" Hale to Zipp Newman to the Jackson, Mississippi newspaper sports editor Jimmy McDowell, December 30, 1959.

[16] Robert K. Brannon, Sr. letter to Jimmy McDowell, December 30, 1959.

[17] http://msfame.com/hall-of-fame/inductees/e-w-goat-hale/

The 1950s

1960s

Introduction

By 1960 the population of Birmingham had grown four percent to 340,887 from 1950. Alabama's largest city was the center of many events around the state and an attraction for conventions and sports. *The Birmingham News* held wide circulation and had a good regional as well as local reputation as a news outlet. Social problems, however, lurked. Civil trouble was developing.

Zipp's workload in his retirement seems to have increased and other observers of his career concur. His work continued at his own initiative. He continued to write letters on company stationery, but instead of the downtown newspaper address, his letterhead carried his home address.

There is also a shift in Zipp's articles and letter writing. Although somewhat present in his writings in the 1950s, one can see a shift toward recollection and reflection. Friendship became deeper as old men wrote about and to one another. Halls of Fame were becoming important and numerous, and friends of candidates petitioned Zipp, knowing of his widespread influence with virtually every sports institution in the nation.

Civil Unrest in Birmingham

The most distressing aspect of the early 1960s in Birmingham were the problems revolving around Civil Rights. Unrest in the city affected everyone and when the Sixteenth Street Baptist Church was bombed on that fateful Sunday morning, killing four young African-American girls, not only Birmingham, but the nation and the world were angered and torn apart.

The Campaign for Civil Rights began in April of 1963, and in mid-April the "Letter from a Birmingham Jail" was penned by the Reverend Dr. Martin Luther King, Jr. Street riots occurred in early May, and then the bombing of the church in September 1963. It would take decades to find and convict the perpetrators of the bombing. Birmingham had to work hard to overcome its tainted reputation. Birmingham had to learn how to deal with its own situation.

Surrounding that terrible situation, other events and activities continued. Nationally, the Salk vaccine for polio was replaced and upgraded by the Sabin vaccine. Polio, suddenly, is no longer an issue. In the sports world Zipp Newman began receiving letters and telephone calls from boosters and promoters of former sports stars, petitioning him for recommendations to their respective halls of fame.

Lest We Forget

Newman wrote, from time to time, articles in *Coach and Athlete Magazine* about athletes and coaches from the past in "Lest We Forget." Old friends began nominating not just athletes for the halls of fame, but persons to remember in *"Lest We Forget."*

Dr. Lenox Baker, Director of Physical Education and Athletics at Duke University wrote to Zipp on May 10, 1966, thanking him for his article about Daniel Earl McGugin. He noted that he had read sometime earlier another *Lest We Forget* about Wallace Wade. Before going to Duke University, Baker was a trainer at the University of Tennessee during R.R. Neyland's first four years.

When he moved to Duke University in Durham, North Carolina, Baker wrote that he had the good fortune of working first with Jimmy DeHart and then with Wallace Wade. Jimmy DeHart was head football coach at Duke from 1926 to 1930, Wade from 1931 to 1941.

Baker wrote that "For many years I have had a great respect for you. ... One of the best friends and greatest admirers you ever had was [University of Tennessee head football coach] Robert R. Neyland."[1]

Twenty days later Baker again wrote to Zipp, thanking him for his letter of May 26. Zipp wanted information from Baker on the "old timers" Russ Cohen and Jimmy DeHart before writing a *Lest We Forget* article on the "General" R.R. Neyland.[2]

Single-Wing and "T" Formations

Cohen taught all of the great coaches the single-wing football formation, although Pop Warner created it. Dr. Baker wrote Zipp that Jimmy DeHart, who learned the single-wing under Warner when a player at the University of Pittsburgh, told him that:

"Russ Cohen knew more about [that formation] than anyone and could find defects in [an offensive] attack quicker than anyone."

Clark Shaughnessy also read Zipp's article about McGugin. He wrote to Zipp on May 16, 1966, to tell him so.[3] Shaughnessy was the college football coach credited with designing the "T" formation. He coached at Tulane University, University of Chicago, Loyola-New Orleans, Stanford, Maryland, Hawaii, and in the National Football League with the Los Angeles Rams. His college football playing days were at the University of Minnesota.

Shaughnessy's best coaching year was 1940. In his first year at Stanford, his team went undefeated at 9-0 and won the 1941 Rose Bowl game. Earlier in the year he assisted in preparing the Chicago Bears to a 73-0 National Football League Championship game over the Washington Redskins.[4] Shaughnessy and Newman corresponded for years and became good friends.

Newman wrote a *Lest We Forget* article about Shaughnessy, published in the December 1967 issue of *Coach and Athlete Magazine*.[5] Shaughnessy thanked Zipp for writing the article – "... It was most flattering." Shaughnessy continued in his thank you letter, telling Zipp:

> "The National Football Foundation, as you undoubtedly know by this time, has put me in their Hall of Fame. I never expected this honor because I sort of assumed that my long connection with the pros [professional football] would have disqualified me. I am quite sure that your article had a lot to do with that award." [6]

Southern Living Magazine opened its facility in Birmingham in 1966 as did the Southern Museum of Flight.

Connections
A letter from Zipp Newman to Dwight Keith contains no date and shows only "Wednesday."

> "Dear Dwight – I appreciate all the Hall of Fame Information you sent me. I don't know when the Governor [George C. Wallace] can get around to it – so heavily involved in our racial problems. I have more than 200 names to submit – Alabama has had it's [sic] share of top people in sports since the Civil War. I enjoyed our visit learning some things I needed to know. I have asked the office to mail you a half dozen tear sheets. And I wish to congratulate you on your

The 1960s

magazine [*Coach and Athlete*] – keep up the good work. Sincerely, Zipp."7

Despite its uncharacteristic looseness, this letter to Dwight Keith is important on several levels. Apparently Zipp learned much from Keith about the beginnings of the *Georgia Sports Hall of Fame*. Keith was instrumental in its founding. In his eagerness to create a hall for Alabama, Zipp conducted research and asked questions of many other halls of fame founders.

In one of his *"Dusting 'Em Off"* columns, Newman wrote on May 21, 1963, about "his friend, Dwight Keith." The article began:

> "Name the field in sports and you have an Alabama boy who reached lofty peaks. No Alabama boy had ever had a finer training as an athlete and coach to own, publish and edit a magazine devoted to the technical side of sports than Dwight Keith. For 25 years he has published Coach and Athlete, circulated in all the colleges and high schools of the country."8

Zipp wrote that it was Wallace Wade who gave Dwight Keith his opportunity to coach in a clinic, and Georgia Tech's Coach Bill Alexander who named him to his coaching staff in 1941. It appears that Zipp's article could have been an attempt to promote the Argo, Alabama native's chances of election into the *Alabama Sports Hall of Fame* without saying so. Nevertheless, Keith's career achievements remained evident.

Dwight Keith and Zipp Newman were Southern sports journalist colleagues. Keith, over his career, was a football coach at the high school and academy levels in Alabama and college in Georgia. Dwight Keith has never been inducted into the *Alabama Sports Hall of Fame*.

Lawrence Wood Robert, Jr. wrote to Zipp on February 28, 1966, to thank him for his cordial letter. The two men traveled with the Georgia Tech football team to the 1929 Rose Bowl Game. Both received special Georgia Tech Rose Bowl wristwatches – Zipp for his reporting and Robert as Chairman of the Athletic Committee for Georgia Tech.

Robert, a 1908 graduate of Georgia Tech, founded what developed to be a successful Atlanta-based engineering and architectural firm, *Robert and Company*. Robert wrote in his letter to Zipp that Georgia Tech people are "distressed" at losing [Arthur Marvin] "Tonto" Coleman. Coleman, born in the small town of Phil Campbell, Alabama, was a football coach at Abilene Christian College in Texas and the University of Florida before going to Georgia Tech. Robert was distressed because Coleman was leaving to replace Bernie Moore as Commissioner of the Southeastern Conference, but elated over his election.

In Zipp's letter to Robert, he apparently asked about the great golfer Bobby Jones. "... I see him almost every Sunday at home when Mrs. Robert and I go by to visit at lunchtime when we are in Atlanta." Jones had become crippled as he aged but Robert noted that Jones's mind still worked wonderfully.

Robert said that he would take great pleasure in letting Jones know that Zipp Newman recalled that the first tournament won by Jones outside the State of Georgia was in Roebuck, a suburban area of Birmingham, Alabama. [9]

Influence, Nominations, Networking

Persons involved with sports, especially when their participation is at what is considered a high level, overtly or privately, wish to be inducted into the hall of fame. Clem Sehrt, President of the National American Bank in New Orleans wrote to Newman on June 9, 1966, in support of William Elton "Bucky" Moore of McComb, Mississippi for the Football Hall of Fame. Sehrt learned of Moore's possible nomination from his good friend Clark Shaughnessy and knew that Zipp possessed a measure of influence in the nominating process. [10]

Sehrt's letter to Zipp covered in some detail Moore's accomplishments as a college player, semi-professional player, and as a coach. Zipp probably already had a folder on Bucky Moore's accomplishments.

This letter, like many others, appears to be one of the avenues of networking developed over the years as great sports figures became eligible for admission into statewide or national sports halls of fame. Zipp Newman, the well-established sports editor and writer, was petitioned not only by individual persons supporting their best friend or favorite sports personality, but by organizations that polled him for names he considered noteworthy for any year's lists of nominees. Zipp was at the center of activity surrounding all sports.

In the years between Robert Brannon's first letter to Zipp in 1959 and his letter to Zipp on February 12, 1968, "Goat" Hale had been inducted

The 1960s

77

into the National Football Hall of Fame. Brannon wrote his letter of thanks to Zipp because "Goat" told Brannon that "you [Zipp] did much to get him named to the National Hall of Fame."

Brannon's handwritten letter updated Zipp on the relationship between him and Hale. Writing that "Goat" was in great shape at seventy-one years old and weighed three pounds less than when he played at Mississippi College. "Goat" retired from his sporting goods business. Brannon believed that Zipp would want to have this latest update on Hale.[11]

Forrest Hood "Fob" James, Jr. served two terms as Governor of Alabama from 1979 to 1983 and from 1995 to 1999. After graduating from prep school at the famed Baylor School in Chattanooga, Tennessee, James attended Auburn University and played football under legendary coach Ralph "Shug" Jordan.

Newman wrote an article in *The Birmingham News* about James in early March 1968. James wrote a thank you letter saying, "I deeply appreciate your kind words ..."[12] James owned *Diversified Products Corporation* in Opelika, Alabama, a town not far from Auburn.

James reminded Zipp that Billy Hitchcock and he were holding him to

> "your promise to make a trip down to Opelika from Birmingham to visit with your country friends. We even know where a couple of good fishing holes are, and we want you to try your hand here, too."

There are several fish-related stories in Zipp's history. The letter was signed Fob James, Jr.

Roy B. Sewell, then president of his clothing manufacturing company in Bremen, Georgia, wrote to Zipp thanking him for mailing him a copy of the *Book of Common Prayer*. The letter was written on April 19, 1968. Zipp attended the *Episcopal Church of the Advent* in downtown Birmingham. Sewell was a member of the *Second Ponce de Leon Baptist Church* in Atlanta. Sewell felt compelled to tell Zipp that his Sunday School lessons for the last quarter were on the book of Hebrews. This letter is an indicator of the developing relationship between the two men.[13]

The 1960s

A few days later Zipp received a letter from Charles Brooks of the editorial staff at *The Birmingham News,* inviting him to "become an honorary member of the newly formed Birmingham Press Club." The April 19 letter informed Zipp of the time of the ceremonies and that several media organizations would cover the event. Certainly, it was an honor to be invited into the new organization as an "honorary" member, but it is difficult to grasp why no regular membership was offered, given Zipp's wide-ranging journalistic accomplishments. Zipp was still writing articles and writing letters. Perhaps the honorary status was due to Zipp's "retired" status. Nonetheless, Zipp received his membership along with others on April 24 at the 1:30pm gathering.[14]

Alabama Recreation

Zipp wrote a series of articles about family recreation in the State of Alabama, mentioning many of the lakes created by the Alabama Power Company. Hydro-electric power generated from dammed rivers produced the beautiful lakes and recreational facilities still evident in the state. Joe Farley, the executive vice president of Alabama Power wrote,

> "Your articles in the last several Sunday papers on Alabama Power Company reservoirs have been most interesting to me and to many others. I most appreciate your writing this series and can assure you that we who work for the company are grateful for your interest and your articles."[15]

The articles not only promoted the many outdoor sporting activities becoming available in Alabama, but Newman identified Alabama Power Company as the responsible corporate citizen for creating hydro-electric power and the many family recreational areas that came from it, like dam-created lakes.

Other Letters

Bill Nichols, U.S. Congressman of the 4th District in Alabama, which is the Anniston area, wrote on July 12, 1968, in appreciation of Zipp's letter regarding a "mutual tribute to our friend, Don Drennen." The Congressman also brought to Zipp's attention Dr. Walter B. Jones.

Jones was the State Geologist of Alabama and was retired at the time of this letter. According to Nichols, Jones is a great storyteller and could tell Zipp of his interest in gold – gold in Chilton County. "He has two bags of it stashed away for his children."[16]

Ralph "Shug" Jordan, on July 23, 1968, wrote to Zipp thanking him for his letter when Shug was seriously ill.[17]

It Suits Me

Roy B. Sewell wrote to Zipp that he likes the fancy stationery of his last letter. He informed Zipp that he and his wife were planning to fly to Birmingham for the Auburn-Georgia Tech game on October 19, 1968, at Legion Field, a game that Auburn lost 20-21, and hoped to visit with Zipp at that time ... "I am going by the *Guest House* Saturday morning." Sewell said that he planned to see the Miami-Auburn game in Auburn, the Auburn-Tennessee game, and the Auburn-Alabama game.

Sewell had for several years tried to give Zipp a business suit that Sewell Manufacturing produced. Apparently Zipp accepted. Sewell in this letter of October 12, 1968, said that he "[w]as delighted to get your letter and glad you liked the suit." [18]

Allen Davis wrote to Zipp on November 13, 1968, saying he would send, under separate cover, a copy of *Sports Illustrated* with an interesting story about "Bo" McMillan on page 73. Handwritten on stationery of Davis Brothers Farm of Danville, Kentucky. The author of the article, Davis asserted, "embellished the story in several places but generally the facts are correct."

Davis tells Zipp that Bo McMillan was not ignorant but smart and like "many athletes did not study after graduations, as you may know, he was a much greater speaker than many coaches."[19]

McMillan played football at Centre College in Danville, Kentucky alongside many other college football greats such as Red Roberts, Sully Montgomery and Red Weaver. He coached college football at Centenary, Geneva, Kansas State and Indiana. His professional coaching took him to the Detroit Lions and then to the Philadelphia Eagles. Having a winning percentage in college football and a losing professional record, McMillan was wrongly criticized in the article to which Davis alluded.

This letter to Zipp might have been a positioning letter, meaning that even though McMillan had played football more than forty-five years earlier, the legacy of McMillan needed to be accurate. Davis probably knew or at least sensed that any future "correction" in a sports story about

The 1960s

McMillan written by Zipp Newman would certainly set the record straight.

Tallulah

W.H. Hutsell, long-time track coach at Auburn University, and Zipp Newman exchanged letters for years. The uniqueness of Hutsell's letters was that he always, with the exception of one, opened his letters with *"Dear Henry"* and closed with *"Wilbur."* And for some years Hutsell wrote his letters on the Auburn University official stationery of James Ralph "Shug" Jordan.

On January 28, 1969, Hutsell wrote Zipp that he had been intending

> "to drop you a line ever since the papers carried so much on Tallulah Bankhead's death. Just wanted to ask if you remembered that she and her dad sat on the Auburn bench at our first game in West Point—or it might have been the second. Her presence may have caused you and me to miss a couple of plays."[20]

Hutsell closed his two-paragraph letter by congratulating Zipp on the impressive line-up of inductees for the upcoming Hall of Fame induction and lamenting the fact that he could not attend because he would be in Montgomery refereeing in the State High School Meet.[21]

Alabama Sports Hall of Fame

In 1965 Zipp Newman met with University of Alabama All-America football player Holt Rast, who was then a member of the Alabama State Legislature. This was the beginning of the legislative process that would create the State of Alabama Sports Hall of Fame (ASHOF).

From 1939 to 1941 Rast played end under coach Frank Thomas, was a unanimous All-America selection in 1941, and was voted Most Valuable Player in the 1942 Cotton Bowl. Although drafted by the Chicago Bears, Rast never played professional football but served in the U.S. Army in World War II and was a highly decorated soldier.[22] Alabama Governor George Wallace appointed Rast to work on the development of the Alabama Sports Hall of Fame.

Frank "Pig" House, a retired major leaguer, became the Alabama Sports Hall of Fame's first board chairman; Allyn McKeen of

Montgomery, vice-chair; Tram Sessions of Birmingham, secretary-treasurer; and Zipp the organization's first executive secretary.[23]

Zipp Newman was inducted into the Alabama Sports Hall of Fame in 1975. Rast in 1977.

Zipp Newman's Typewriter
Alabama Sports Hall of Fame & Museum

First Induction Dinner Alabama Sports Hall of Fame

The first induction dinner for the Alabama Sports Hall of Fame occurred on February 7, 1969. The impressive line-up as referenced in Hutsell's earlier letter were Jesse Owens, Hank Aaron, Joe Louis, Willie Mays, and Carl Lewis.[24] Days later Zipp received letters of congratulations and appreciation for the Hall of Fame's inauguration.

Torance "Bo" Russell, who would be inducted into the Alabama Sports Hall of Fame in 1979, wrote to Zipp. Offering his "sincere congratulations" Russell noted that without Zipp's efforts the Alabama Sports Hall of Fame would not have become a reality. "

> "I know that Friday night was a real wonderful answer to a number of dreams you have had over the years."

Russell played football at Auburn University and was outstanding as a freshman player. In 1938 he reached All-Star status as captain, and his teammates voted him player of the year. After playing professional football for the Washington Redskins he worked with the Massachusetts Mutual Life Insurance Company in Birmingham. His letter of

The 1960s

appreciation to Zipp was typed on company stationery on February 11, 1969.[25]

Zipp received a copy of a letter from Jimmie McDowell addressed to Earle Edwards, the football coach at North Carolina State University, dated February 11, 1969. Zipp must have received it a few days later. Of note were the carbon copy (cc) names: Bill Murray, Bob Woodruff, Fred Sington, William Winter, Dwight Keith, Reed Green and Roy Clogston. Although the letter was typed, a handwritten note read: "Fred, could you mail Earle [a] copy of Alabama Sports Hall of Fame rules? Jimmie." Then the names Frank House and Zipp Newman handwritten in numerator-denominator fashion below that of "Jimmie."

It is interesting to read the names of House and Newman handwritten at the bottom left of the letter. Frank "Pig" House,[26] a native of Bessemer, Alabama, was a major league catcher for the Detroit Tigers, Kansas City Athletics, and the Cincinnati Reds. After baseball he was elected to the Alabama Legislature where he, along with Rast, was pivotal in creating the Alabama Sports Hall of Fame with Newman.

Jimmie McDowell at the time of this letter was Director of Public Relations at *The National Football Foundation and Hall of Fame*. He worked from the New Brunswick, New Jersey Office. McDowell said that he enclosed a copy of the National Football Hall of Fame nomination blank for Earle Edwards and wrote that its formula for nomination "is that a player has to be out of college 10 years and a coach is not eligible until he has been out three years."

Earle Edwards was seeking assistance in establishing a *North Carolina State University Hall of Fame* on campus. In the letter McDowell mentioned that the *National Football Foundation and Hall of Fame* (NFF/HOF) chapter presidents would send him their requirements. He listed them by name: William Winter of the *Mississippi Sports Hall of Fame*; Bob Woodruff of the *Tennessee Sports Hall of Fame*; Fred Sington of the *Alabama Sports Hall of Fame*; and Dwight Keith of the *Georgia Sports Hall of Fame*. Also listed was Reed Green of *Mississippi Southern University*, who with the other chapter presidents would forward copies of their organizing history and their rules for inductees.

McDowell said that "On-campus recognition can also be a step in the right direction for national recognition. I see no conflict whatsoever, and, as a matter of fact, one group helps the other, stimulating interest in amateur athletics."[27]

Herbert "Bones" Farr, of the Auburn football class of 1914, wrote that the inaugural ASHOF banquet was beautifully organized and well done. He was, however, disappointed in the "utter neglect" of John E. "Boozer" Pitts.

Farr wrote further about Pitts' medical problem with his throat, his military service in World War I and World War II and that he was a full-bird colonel in the Army. In effect, Farr was nominating Pitts for future induction to the Alabama Sports Hall of Fame.

> "I do not need to tell you anything about John Pitts – All American Football Center, Football Coach, Mathematics Genius and Teacher for thirty years, Full Colonel U.S. Army with service in World War I and II and Author."[28]

This was yet another letter testifying to the influence of Zipp Newman in future picks for the hall of fame. A mark of high respect.

James B. Pratt of Birmingham wrote a Valentine's Day note in 1969 to congratulate Zipp on the first Alabama Sports Hall of Fame gathering. Pratt wrote that he was glad to see that his uncle, Derrill Pratt, was one of the nominees.[29]

George W. Seibels, Mayor of Birmingham, sent a congratulatory letter to Frank House for all the work done on behalf of the *Alabama Sports Hall of Fame*. "The attendance, I feel, was a tribute to you and the hard work on the part of those who assisted you."[30] The letter was copied to all Board Members of the Alabama Sports Hall of Fame.

Goose Dinner

Cecil B. Word was president of the W.J. Word Lumber Company of Scottsboro, Alabama, a city in the northeast corner of the state. Within a few days of the first induction ceremonies of the new *Alabama Sports Hall of Fame*, Word congratulated Zipp Newman for his many wonderful Humanitarian Projects.

Word observed Newman's work over the years and in a letter to him noted that he had given a lot of time, energy and thought in helping to make other people happy. He grouped Zipp with similar-serving people such as Dick Cavaleri and Dr. John Sherrill. A handwritten line at the bottom of this letter of February 13, 1969, read,

> "I want to get with you and Dick [Cavaleri] soon and work on the Goose Dinner before Spring practice."[31]

Newman wrote to his buddy Hutsell about the Goose Dinner, but he also inquired about setting up a meeting with Dr. Homer Swingle. Hutsell's response to Zipp said that the Goose Dinner sounded mighty good, but that Scottsboro is a long way from Saugahatchee Creek.[32] He also responded to Zipp's request for a meeting with Dr. Homer Swingle, a professor at Auburn University who was not only an entomologist but an avid fisherman. One can only guess why Zipp wanted to meet with him. [33] It was not about a fishing outing.

Swingle discovered that despite Alabama's rich water resources, pond fishing did not meet his standards, so he and a colleague recognized the necessity of water impoundment as a means of water storage for the production of food, and for recreation.[34] Hutsell told Zipp that getting up with Swingle was difficult because he was one busy man. We must assume that Newman eventually met with Swingle and that such a meeting was fruitful.

There is a Goose Pond in Scottsboro which is city-owned. Its current-day promotion reads as follows:

> *"Located on the banks of the Tennessee River's beautiful Lake Guntersville and nestled into the picturesque Cumberland Mountains, Goose Pond Colony Resort awaits your arrival. Goose Pond Colony is a municipally owned resort that will take your breath away. With two beautiful 18-hole championship golf courses, comfortable lakeside cottages, lodge, relaxing waterfront campground, walking trail, full service marina, meeting facilities, The Docks Restaurant, swimming pool, beach area and Lake Guntersville, we are all you need for a relaxing vacation or one day outing."* [35]

Cecil Word probably culled the name from his Scottsboro surroundings and it was a way to attract sportsmen to his area. We could not locate the record of the first Goose Dinner, but June 8, 1972, serves as an example. The Goose Dinners became an annual event.

The 1960s

Richard Thigpen, at the time Executive Assistant to the President of The University of Alabama, wrote to Zipp after the June 8th dinner:

> "Dear Mr. Newman: It was a pleasure to visit briefly with you at the annual goose dinner in Scottsboro sponsored by Mr. Cecil Word. Needless to say, we at The University of Alabama take great pride in this annual occasion, since, as Mr. Cavaleri indicated, it has its origin in an effort by yourself and others to raise funds for our crippled children's clinic program in Birmingham."

Thigpen added that the University has never forgotten the wonderful efforts by Newman and that the University leadership takes great pride in their association with him.[36]

On February 26, 1973, Cecil Word sent invitations for the next Goose Dinner. Word and Thigpen visited briefly in February at the annual *Alabama Sports Hall of Fame* induction dinner. Thigpen wrote to Word that he had received the invitation and looked forward to the dinner planned for April 24, 1973.

The next year, 1974, Zipp Newman wrote a letter to Thigpen and in his last paragraph mentioned the upcoming Goose Dinner planned for June 6 or June 13. More importantly, Zipp had other events to cite, and as was characteristically Zipp, he congratulated Thigpen on his promotion from Executive Assistant to the President of the University of Alabama to Executive Vice President. Zipp also extended his and Mr. Word's gratitude to Thigpen and University President Mathews for the attention and courtesy shown to them at the recent A-Day Game.[37] Thigpen followed with a return letter dated May 23, thanking Zipp for his kind words and saying that he was looking forward to the Goose Dinner and hoped to see Zipp there.[38]

In all likelihood Zipp Newman was the organizer or the concept-developer of Scottsboro's Goose Dinner. Cecil B. Word was its sponsor and on-going operator of the event.

Zipp's Research and His Sources

Gabriel Howard Paul, known as Gabe, was a long-term general manager of four major league professional baseball clubs – the Cincinnati Reds, the Houston Colt .45s (which became the Houston Astros in 1964), the Cleveland Indians, and the New York Yankees. Zipp Newman wrote to Paul, then general manager of the Cleveland Indians, asking for information and pictures of selected Alabama baseball players for the *Alabama Sports Hall of Fame*.

Zipp wanted pictures of Joe Sewell and Luke Sewell, and Tris Speaker. Paul replied in a letter dated May 16, 1969 that he would send pictures under separate cover.

Joe Sewell was an infielder for the Indians and the Yankees and was inducted into major league baseball's hall of fame in 1977. He was born in an unincorporated Elmore County, Alabama community known as Titus, in 1898. Sewell attended the University of Alabama and played minor league baseball in New Orleans before being called to the majors. Joe Sewell lived to be 91.

Joe's brother, James Luther "Luke" Sewell, also played at the University of Alabama. He played AA baseball in Columbus, Ohio, and then with the majors at Cleveland, Washington Senators, Chicago White Sox, and the St. Louis Browns. He coached at St. Louis and Cincinnati. Luke lived to age 86.

Joe and Luke Sewell's younger brother Tommy played for the Chicago Cubs in 1927. He was hitless as a pinch hitter in one at-bat. He died at age 50. Luke Sewell was inducted into the *Alabama Sports Hall of Fame* in the Class of 1973 in the category of Distinguished Sportsmen.[39] Joe Sewell was inducted in the Class of 1970 in the category of Distinguished Sportsmen.[40]

Zipp received the requested pictures from Gabe Paul. The two men continued their correspondence over the years. Paul wrote to Zipp that "If I get to Birmingham, I will certainly look up ole Zipp." Paul added that "It was so nice to hear from you. What we need now is some Burgundy!"[41]

The Third Saturday in October

Tom Siler of *The Knoxville News-Sentinel* wrote to Zipp on May 16, 1969, apparently in reply to an earlier letter from Zipp. "The poll is completed. But I don't want to say anything more about it." Siler might have been referencing a poll of All-Star athletes, but it is uncertain.

Zipp knew how to write an exciting article. In April 1969 Nash Buckingham wrote to Newman about the Tennessee-Alabama 6-6 tie, noting that an Alabama friend had mailed to him Zipp's "recent recounting of Tennessee's battle royal with Alabama, Thanksgiving Day, 1901."[42] It was the first ever game between the two schools, played at

Birmingham's West End Park. Oddly, the rivalry became known as *"The Third Saturday in October,"* a nomenclature that ended in 1992.[43] Buckingham played for Tennessee in that 1901 game.

Without comment, Siler inserted a newspaper clipping, perhaps from the *News-Sentinel*, about an article penned by Newman. The clipping opened with "ZIPP NEWMAN, sports editor emeritus of *The Birmingham News*, recalled the other day that Tennessee-Alabama 6-6 tie in 1901. He wrote of the stirring deeds that day of Nash Buckingham, the Vols fullback well-known to many Tennessee fans, especially Memphians since he has lived there for so long." Zipp wrote that the game was called on account of darkness, Buckingham averred.[44]

The sun was bright when the game was called, as Buckingham remembered, so darkness is a "misconception." Buckingham wrote that his Tennessee team was in Alabama territory and about to score when Buckingham was "headed off by spectators." The referee took the ball and began fending off the crowd – a crowd of gamblers and alumni, wrote Buckingham – and called an end to the game but declared it "forfeited." The next thing Nash knew was that the Tennessee football team was surrounded by "Mack Sennett cops"[45] and escorted off the field.

Zipp and Buckingham would continue their correspondence through the years. Buckingham was a great outdoorsman and wrote many books. Perhaps his most famous book was *De Shootinest Gent'man & Other Tales*.

On June 3, 1969, Sam Bailey, Associate Director of Athletics, University of Alabama, wrote a thank you letter to Zipp who had written congratulations on Bailey's new position.[46] Zipp Newman understood that teams are not simply composed of athletic directors, coaches, assistant coaches, and players. College administrators, assistant administrators, team trainers, sports officials, sportswriters, and sports fans also contribute to the enjoyment of sports. Zipp let them know they were appreciated for their work.

Four Men in a Boat

There was a boat-sinking event in the past, and Zipp included his recollection of it – since he was there – in an article published in *The Birmingham News* on June 15, 1969. It did not take long for his friend at Auburn University, W.H. "Wilbur" Hutsell, to update Zipp's memory.

Zipp, Hutsell, and former Alabama football coach Red Drew, a Tallapoosa County, Alabama native, and Auburn University graduate Beverly Holstun, were the four men.

A noted agricultural leader and Extension chairman in his home county as well as Tuscaloosa County, Holstun served in World War II as an economics officer in the Army, curbing black market commodities in several sectors of Germany.[47]

Red Drew's college years in Maine and Massachusetts were interrupted by his service in World War I as a naval aviator.[48]

Wilbur Hutsell, a Mobley, Missouri native, was named track coach at Auburn University in 1921 after three years as assistant track coach at the University of Missouri. He was on the Olympic coaching staffs in 1924, 1928, and 1932. Hutsell was inducted into the *Alabama Sports Hall of Fame* in 1970 in the category Distinguished Sportsmen.[49]

Hutsell's response to Zipp's article recalls that their fishing outing was conducted at night, and it was raining slightly. It was about 9:30pm and the boat was overloaded. Hutsell sat in the middle of the craft, holding to both sides, when suddenly the waves began to slap against his fingers.

Drew, using marine lingo, declared, "mates she is sinking." Minutes later Drew directed, "mates, don't abandon shop 'til she hits bottom," which happened shortly thereafter. [50] Hutsell recalled that he "thought that we had been paddling towards the middle, but learned we were just paralleling the shoreline, which made for a more pleasant landing."[51]

Newman, Drew, Holstun, and Hutsell – a sports journalist, head football coach, agricultural extension officer and a former college track coach, respectively – enjoyed each other's company. All were sportsmen. Yes, in a sense one could attribute the outing as one among the "good ole boys." Each man had his own direction and purpose. All loved fishing, and all wanted to stay in touch. It was one node in human networking.

A Decade into Retirement

By 1969 Zipp Newman had been retired for ten years but no one paid attention to it, not even Zipp. As Sports Editor Emeritus Zipp simply continued his career, mostly from his home. His stationery letterhead still displayed *The Birmingham News*, but his home on Montevallo Road was the mailing address.

The 1960s

With decades of journalistic and organizational achievements, Zipp was still polled for his thoughts about sports and humanitarian concerns. The public information officer of the Southeastern Conference, Elmore Hudgins, wrote to Zipp in July of 1969 informing him that he had been selected as one of a committee of seven to make the final selection of the All-Time football teams for the Southeast Area.[52]

In addition to Newman, the other journalists selected were Jack Hairston of the *Jacksonville* [Florida] *Journal*; Jesse Outler of the *Atlanta Constitution;* Cawood Ledford of WHAS Radio in Kentucky; Bud Montet of the *Baton Rouge Advocate*; Carl Walters of the *Jackson* [Mississippi], *Clarion-Ledger*; and Raymond Johnson of the *Nashville Tennessean.*

Two weeks later Newman heard from *The Football Writers Association of America* (FWAA) and its Secretary-Treasurer, Bert McGrane.[53] McGrane began his letter with,

"Get out of that rocking chair and get busy. We need your help."

America's football Centennial was the year 1969 and the FWAA was preparing a Press Kit to apprise the general media of the event to be held in New York City at a black-tie dinner.

The Press Kit would contain stories about the All-Time America team. Actually, it was to be teams because the selections were to be based on an Early Day players' team from 1869 to 1919 and the Modern Day team from 1919 to 1969. Zipp's assignment was to write a story dealing only with the first team tackles from the Modern Team. Players like Bronko Nagurski of Minnesota or Bruiser Kinard of Ole Miss.

For his story Zipp was guaranteed $150.00, and even though McGrane's letter was dated August 3, he gave a deadline of August 15, 1969.

And the Band Played On
The Jacksonville [Alabama] State University Band received a "plug" written by Zipp in early August 1969. The article caused the President of the University to send Zipp a note of institutional and personal appreciation for his kind words. President Houston Cole wrote that,

"The plug you gave could materialize in an invitation to one of the bowl games at the first of the year."

Cole went on to tell Newman that the university band "has been chosen by the American Bowl in Tampa for a permanent performance at its games" and that the band director had been asked to compose the marching song for the annual event.[54]

The Book

Zipp Newman had been working on a book for some time – a book of sports statistics and famous personalities in sports. The book's content would not be limited to the South, despite its pending title *The Impact of Southern Football*. Although the book was not published until 1969, word got out and Zipp's friends in New Orleans were a step ahead.

The "Sugar Bowlers" in New Orleans, officially known as the *New Orleans Mid-Winter Sports Association*, wished to procure signed copies of the book. Edna D. Engert, the Executive Secretary of the Association, wrote to the publisher of Zipp's book, Morros & Associates in Montgomery, Alabama. In her October 11, 1969, letter Engert opened with "We would like to have a copy of Mr. Newman's book for our office library" with a directive that the book was to be forwarded to Mr. Newman for his personalization. She also asked that Mr. Newman "insert a personal message to the Sugar Bowlers."[55]

Zipp Newman's football scoring sheet that he developed and promoted early in his career, flew with little success. In fact, it did not fly at all. After getting his scoring sheet copyrighted, he mailed copies of it to dozens of college football head coaches, college administrators, and colleagues. But he learned from that experience.

His book, *The Impact of Southern Football*, was promoted months before it was released. Newman mailed copies to many people, but it never was a bestseller – it would be today, if rescued from hibernation. Zipp received favorable comments about his book, which varied broadly and came in the form of letters. The book is a mix of statistics, facts not generally known, and short biographies.

From Google Images

A.M. "Tonto" Coleman, who was Commissioner of the Southeastern Conference from 1966 to 1972, wrote to Zipp saying that his book was a

> "veritable goldmine ... Certainly you've done a thrilling job in describing the gridiron exploits of yesterday's hero but, in addition, you've been magnificent in giving credit and in paying honor and respect to those who were the founders, architects and builders of this splendid program ..."

Coleman touched on the heart of Newman's writings – Zipp Newman always showed respect for people in whatever endeavor they pursued. But the book, according to Coleman, was exacting, chronological, and encyclopedic.[56] That was an interesting and correct comment by Coleman. Zipp's scoring sheet received varying comments, most of which praised the high value of the sheet and its many uses not just by coaches but by fans who did not know the game of football. Unfortunately for Zipp, neither his scoring sheet nor his *Impact* book succeeded with wide distribution. Compliments, however, kept coming in from those in the know of sports.

On August 21, 1969, John F. Hendon of Birmingham, owner of an auto parts storage company, wrote to Bill Streit, thanking him for presenting him with a copy of Zipp's new book.

> "I am amazed at the tremendous volume of statistics ..."

Streit, a native of Birmingham, in his college days played tackle at Auburn University and then at Washington and Lee College in Virginia.[57]

Several people purchased Zipp's book, not only for themselves but as gifts for friends. One gift recipient was Richard M. Nixon.

The President of the United States wrote to Zipp on October 23, 1969, saying how delighted he was to have a copy of *Impact*.

"I have seen several of those Rose Bowl Games you describe so vividly."[58]

One wonders how President Nixon received his copy. The book was not a gift from Newman.

Men's clothing manufacturer Roy B. Sewell wrote on September 17, 1969, to thank Zipp for a copy of *Impact*. It seems appropriate or at least necessary for authors of books to distribute copies of their books to friends and acquaintances in an effort to stimulate sales. Most of the time, however, it does not work. Nonetheless, recipients of gift books are always grateful.

Zipp also sent Sewell a book celebrating the 100th anniversary of college football, produced by *The Football Writers Association of America*. "You sure are a dandy writer, Zip [sic], and I appreciate you." Sewell asked Zipp for his suit size and preferred color and told him he would send him a "good Sewell" suit.[59]

Jess Neely, of Vanderbilt University's Department of Athletics, sent a letter of thanks to Zipp in November of 1969 for his *Impact* book. "I appreciate it more than I can tell you." Neely wrote that the details made him go back and review all the old games and those participating in them. Along with the book gift, Zipp apparently petitioned Neely for his list of Vanderbilt University lettermen.[60]

From Eutaw, Alabama, S.D. "Bull" Bayer, of the University of Tennessee football class of 1916, wrote a lengthy letter to Zipp. The letter was mostly typed but with handwritten notes in the margins and on an additional page. He thanked Zipp for sending a copy of *Impact*. Then he recounted events from his past. His December 19, 1969 letter ended with "I think I should write you again."[61]

W.G. "Pete" Peoples, a consultant with and formerly an executive of Southern Pacific Railroad, wrote on January 20, 1970, that he had just received his copy of *Impact*. "I deeply appreciate receiving this."[62] Peoples wrote a few months earlier to Zipp about the *"Dusting 'Em Off"* article of September 14, 1969. Peoples thought Zipp was generous in what he wrote. But he expressed regret with

> "I am sorry that you cannot attend my retirement dinner on September 30th.[63]

Peoples and Newman had been friends for many years.

Peoples was born in Opp, Alabama and began work at age seventeen for the Louisville & Nashville Railroad in Birmingham and held several clerical positions. In 1920 he joined Southern Pacific as an agent in Birmingham and was transferred to Atlanta in 1925.[64] It is probable that Newman and Peoples met as a result of Newman's travels.

John Sparkman, U.S. Senator from Alabama, wrote Zipp on January 26, 1970,

> "I received the homecoming program that you sent me ... I was glad to see that copy of the letter from the President to you expressing appreciation for the copy of your book that I carried down to him."[65]

Now we learn how President Nixon received his copy of *Impact*. One wonders, had President Nixon mused over Newman and his book *Impact* at a press conference, as did President Ronald Reagan years later over author Tom Clancy and his books, perhaps Zipp would have retired to a mansion on one of Alabama's tranquil lakes.

Larry Klein, Director of the National Collegiate Sports Services, NYC, thanked Zipp for the fine job he did on the All-Time All-America Football team.[66] Klein's gratitude was for the story that Zipp wrote on such a challenging assignment. Zipp's story as well as other contributions by national sportswriters was to be part of a special press kit that the NCSS would send to more than twenty-five hundred sports media people. Klein also asked Zipp to confirm the byline written on his letter. We can assume that Zipp returned his correction to the byline that read "By Zipp

Newman, Birmingham News Sports Editor 1912-64." Klein was off a few years at both ends of the span of years.

Friendships

On September 17, 1969 W.H. Hutsell, Track Coach Emeritus at Auburn University, wrote to Henry Newman, the Sports Editor Emeritus of *The Birmingham News*,

> "Dear Henry: It's not what you know, but who you know, and I'm grateful for your valued friendship of more than 50 years."

He thanked Zipp for carrying the load of the "recent selection" – probably meaning the *Alabama Sports Hall of Fame's* first class. A native of the Midwest, Hutsell wrote that "we" had a fine trip there. And with "a heart full of thanks, and every good wish, Sincerely, Wilbur."[67]

Benny Marshall

One week after Zipp received his letter from Hutsell, Benny Marshall died. Marshall began as a sportswriter for *The Birmingham Age-Herald* in 1939. When Newman retired in 1959, Marshall took over the responsibilities as Sports Editor at *The Birmingham News*.

Benny Marshall was friend to his peers and the sports communities. He was Alabama Sports Writer of the Year seven times and won awards for his writing from the National Sportscasters and Sportswriters Association.

He suffered two heart attacks by the age of 44 and suffered from that during his remaining years. He ended his life with a shotgun. Benny Marshal was inducted into the Alabama Sports Hall of Fame in 1982.[68]

More Letters of Thanks

Mickey O'Brien, Trainer, Department of Athletics, University of Tennessee, thanks Zipp for his article of August 24th mentioning Mickey and other trainers.[69] This letter, written on September 26, 1969, expresses vividly that Zipp did not limit his articles to athletes, coaches, and administrators. Zipp knew the value of trainers and other people who serve sports in a support function.

Dorothy M. Armstrong, Secretary, The National Football Foundation and Hall of Fame, wrote to Zipp on October 7, 1967: "On behalf of Harvey Harman, who is very ill, I wish to thank you very much for the famous

The 1960s

football play diagrams, newspaper clippings, etc. to the Foundation."[70] Zipp had much to donate to institutions such as the National Football Foundation. There is no telling how much material such as play diagrams, game-day programs, articles written about certain persons and letters received, that Zipp did donate.

Charles W. Aiken, President & Founder of Boys Home of the South, Greenville, South Carolina wrote to Zipp at the end of 1969. He referenced Zipp's note to him of May 3, 1969, apparently about the *Alabama Sports Hall of Fame* inaugural ceremonies and dinner. Aiken wanted information about the inaugural dinner. The letter was addressed to Zipp at the Alabama Sports Hall of Fame, 1110 Central Bank Building, Birmingham, perhaps a temporary office until the Hall could be built.

He expressed "great admiration for [Zipp] and your group who have, without a doubt, given much time and effort to a program which seems to be unique and very, very worthwhile.[71] It is not known how the two men met and even though Aiken passed away in Louisville, Kentucky, he was born and lived most of his life in South Carolina. Zipp was not locked in to the South; he was not a writer for southern sports. Zipp was known and respected nationally.

---

[1] Lenox Baker, M.D. Duke University. Typed letter. May 10, 1966.

[2] Lenox Baker, M.D. Memorandum letterhead. May 30, 1966.

[3] Clark Shaughnessy, Los Angeles. Typed, personal letterhead. May 16, 1966.

[4] https://en.wikipedia.org/wiki/Clark_Shaughnessy

[5] Newman. "Lest We Forget – Clark Shaughnessy," *Coach and Athlete*, December 1, 1967, Volume 30, p. 32.

[6] Clark Shaughnessy, Los Angeles. Typed letter on personal letterhead. February 24, 1968.

[7] Zipp Newman letter to Dwight Keith, undated. Typed on The Birmingham News letter with Zipp's home address. Zipp visited Keith probably to learn how the Georgia Sports Hall of Fame got its start. Keith was a founder.

[8] Zipp Newman. "Dusting 'Em Off" column in *The Birmingham News*. May 21, 1963. Article is about the major achievements of Dwight Keith.

[9] Lawrence Wood Robert, Jr. letter to Zipp Newman, February 28, 1966.

[10] Clem H. Sehrt. President, American Bank of New Orleans. Company letterhead. June 9, 1966

[11] Robert L. Brannon, Sr. Montgomery, Alabama. Handwritten letter on personal letterhead. February 12, 1968.

[12] Fob James, Jr. Opelika, Alabama. Typed letter on Diversified Products Corporation letterhead. March 11, 1968.

[13] Roy B. Sewell, Bremen, Georgia. Typed on Sewell Manufacturing Company letterhead. April 10, 1968.

[14] Charles G. Brooks. Editorial Staff. Typed on *The Birmingham News* letterhead. April 19, 1968.

[15] Joseph M. Farley, Executive Vice President, Alabama Power Company, Birmingham, Alabama, May 1, 1968.

[16] Bill Nichols. Congressman from 4th Alabama District. Type on Congressional letterhead. July 12, 1968.

[17] Ralph "Shug" Jordan. Auburn University head football coach. Typed on university letterhead. July 23, 1968.

[18] Roy B. Sewell, Chairman, Sewell Manufacturing Company, Bremen, Georgia. Typed on company letterhead. October 12, 1968.

[19] Allen Davis of Davis Brothers Farm, Danville, Kentucky. Handwritten on company letterhead. November 13, 1968.

[20] Tallulah Bankhead died December 12, 1968 in New York City. See https://en.wikipedia.org/wiki/Tallulah_Bankhead.

[21] W.H. Hutsell. Typed on Auburn University letterhead of James Ralph Jordan. January 28, 1969.

[22] https://en.wikipedia.org/wiki/Holt_Rast

[23] Tom York. Article in Encyclopedia of Alabama online "Alabama Sports Hall of Fame". Last updated February 21, 2014.

[24] http://www.encyclopediaofalabama.org/article/h-1576.

[25] Torance "Bo" A. Russell. Consultant – Massachusetts Mutual Life. Typed on company letterhead. February 11, 1969.

[26] https://en.wikipedia.org/wiki/Frank_House_(baseball).

[27] Jimmie McDowell, Director of Public Relations – The National Football Foundation and Hall of Fame. Letter typed on company letterhead. February 11, 1969.

[28] Herbert "Bones" Farr, Auburn, Alabama. Typed on personal letterhead. February 13, 1969.

[29] James B. Pratt. 10 Office Park, Birmingham, Alabama. Letter type on personal letterhead. February 14, 1969.

[30] George W. Seibels, Jr. Mayor-City of Birmingham, Alabama. Typed letter on city letterhead. March 19, 1969.

[31] Cecil B. Word. W.J. Word Lumber Company, Scottsboro, Alabama. Letter typed on company letterhead with handwritten note at bottom. February 13, 1969.

[32] Saughahatchee Creek flows through western Lee County, Alabama and includes Class I-II waters for kayaking and canoeing. http://www.encyclopediaofalabama.org/article/m-3718.

[33] W.H. Hutsell, Track Coach Emeritus, Auburn University. Typed on university letterhead. February 27, 1969.

[34] http://agriculture.auburn.edu/people/homer-scott-swingle/.

[35] https://www.cityofscottsboro.com/index.php/64-goosepond-colony-resort

[36] Richard Thigpen. Executive Assistant to the President, The University of Alabama. Typed on university letterhead. June 13, 1972.

[37] Zipp Newman to Richard Thigpen. Letter written on stationery of The Birmingham News, Sports Editor Emeritus, May 16, 1974.

[38] Richard Thigpen to Zipp Newman, typed on University of Alabama stationery, Office of the President, May 23, 1974,

[39] http://ashof.org/inductees/baseball/james-luther-sewell

[40] http://ashof.org/inductees/sim-byrd/joseph-wheeler-no-strike-joe-sewell

[41] Gabriel Paul, President, Cleveland Indians Baseball. Typed on company letterhead. May 16, 1969.

[42] Nash Buckingham. Memphis, Tennessee. Typed letter on plain paper. April 29, 1969.

[43] https://en.wikipedia.org/wiki/Third_Saturday_in_October

[44] Tom Siler. Knoxville News-Sentinel. Letter included cut-out article about Zipp.Typed on company letterhead. May 16, 1969.

[45] Meaning "Keystone Cops" https://en.wikipedia.org/wiki/Mack_Sennett.

[46] Sam Bailey, Associate Director of Athletics, University of Alabama. Typed on university letterhead. June 3, 1969.

[47] https://wp.aces.edu/esp/people/holstun-beverly-r/

[48] https://en.wikipedia.org/wiki/Harold_Drew

The 1960s

49 http://ashof.org/inductees/track/wilbur-h-coach-hutsell

50 W.H. Hutsell, Track Coach Emeritus, Auburn University. Typed on university letterhead. June 16, 1969.

51 Ibid

52 Elmore Hudgins, Director of the Puiblic Relations Department at the Southeastern Conference. Typed on conference letterhead. July 15, 1969

53 Bert McGrane, Secretary-Treasurer of The Football Writers Association of America. Typed on organization letterhead. August 3, 1969.

54 Houston Cole. President, Jacksonville State University, Alabama. Typed on university letterhead. August 11, 1969.

55 Edna D. Engert. New Orleans Mid-Winter Sports Association. Typed on corporate letterhead. October 11, 1968

56 A.M. Coleman. Commissioner, Southeastern Conference. Typed on organization letterhead. August 12, 1969.

57 James Franklin Hendon, Birmingham, Alabama. Typed on personal letterhead. August 21, 1969.

58 Richard M. Nixon. The White House. Typed on White House letterhead. October 23, 1969.

59 Roy B. Sewell, Chairman of Sewell Manufacturing Company, Bremen, Georgia. Typed on company letterhead. September 17, 1969.

60 Jess Neely. Department of Athletics, Vanderbilt University. Typed on university letterhead. November 12, 1969.

61 S.D. "Bull" Bayer. Eutaw, Alabama. Football 1916 class, University of Tennessee. Typed on plain paper. December 19, 1969.

62 W.G. Pete Peoples. Consultant. Typed on his personal-business letterhead. January 20, 1970.

63 W.G. Pete Peoples, Senior Vice President, Southern Pacific Company, San Francisco. Typed on company letterhead. September 19, 1969.

64 *Railway Age*, Volume 123, No. 10; September 6, 1947, "W.G. Peoples" history, 78.

65 John Sparkman, United States Senator. Typed on Senate letterhead. January 26, 1970.

66 Larry Klein, Director of the National Collegiate Sports Services, NYC. Typed on organization letterhead. September 5, 1969.

67 W.H. Hutsell, Track Coach Emeritus, Auburn University. Typed on university letterhead. September 17, 1969.

68 https://www.bhamwiki.com/w/Benny_Marshall

69 Mickey O'Brien, Trainer, Department of Athletics, University of Tennessee. Typed on university letterhead. September 26, 1969.

70 Dorothy M. Armstrong, Secretary, The National Football Foundation and Hall of Fame. Typed on foundation letterhead. October 10, 1969.

71 Charles W. Aiken, Greenville, South Carolina. President & Founder of Boys Home of the South. Typed on organization letterhead. December 31, 1969.

The 1960s

1970s

Introduction

Henry Hardin Newman did not slow himself down during his final seven years. He was sought after and encouraged to assist in many programs. Like the 1960s, it was a period of donation for Zipp. Halls of fame, university archives, and public museums received donations from Newman. Many organizations wrote to Zipp, requesting donations of memorabilia.

The decade of the 1970s was filled with accolades for the person Henry Hardin Newman and his work. Zipp and his friends and associates were old men, and given their exchange of letters, the reader would notice that they complained of physical aches and pains while nurturing fond memories.

Birmingham, by 1970, was a major if not the major center of activity in Alabama. With a population of 300,910 Birmingham had a lot of work to do to redeem itself from its history of the early 1960s.

George Gardner, Secretary, Football Officials Association of the Southeastern Conference, wrote to Zipp in early January of 1970 that:

> "We will miss you at our annual party as you have been a big part of it over the years. I can well understand your situation ... I sure hope you fellows have a fine party and will be seeing you along the way."[1]

It should not be surprising to discover that the SEC's football officials and Zipp Newman had a long-running history of interaction. Gardner was an impressive person. A 1925 graduate of Georgia Tech, Gardner earned a Bachelor of Science degree in Civil Engineering. He was elected captain of the Yellow Jacket football team in his senior year. He tried his hand at officiating and loved it and became probably the most authoritative official in college football. He was a referee in the Southeastern Conference and officiated for sixteen years. For the following twenty-eight years Gardner served as supervisor of SEC officials. He was elected to the Georgia Tech Hall of Fame in 1986.[2]

For more than fifty years, Gardner and Newman worked together as avid sportsmen and friends.

William G. Peoples invited Zipp to his retirement party the previous year at a time when Zipp was unable to attend. In January 1970, Peoples received his copy of *The Impact of Southern Football* directly from Zipp who wrote a warm, handwritten tribute to Peoples on the inside cover page. Peoples could not restrain himself in his high respect and admiration for Zipp and returned a thank you letter saying,

> "Throughout the years you have been a staunch friend of mine and a great inspiration to all of us who number you among their friends. You have made your mark at the top of your chosen profession, with honors and awards richly deserved. Your untiring efforts and devotion to the betterment of the underprivileged and other worthwhile cause is admired by all of us.
>
> You have certainly had a very full life and it has been a great privilege and pleasure for me to have your friendship. I enjoyed every minute of the hours and days we have spent together and certainly hope our paths will cross again somewhere very shortly."

Peoples' post script asked Zipp when the book would be on sale so that he could purchase extra copies.

Don E. Liebendorfer was a long-time historian for the Department of Physical Education and Athletics at Stanford University. On January 27, 1970 he sent Zipp two letters: a copy of a letter he wrote to Major Dennis A. Cavagnaro, USMC, about Zipp's column of January 18 and his own letter.[3]

Cavagnaro, [4] an intermediary of sorts, mailed a copy of Zipp's article that he read in South Carolina to Liebendorfer across country in California, who, after reading the article, wrote to Zipp to convey his thanks "for your kindness to Stanford."

Similar to W.H. Hutsell's letter to Zipp, Liebendorfer wrote,

"I must admit that a friendship such as ours, which has endured for nearly half a century, is one of those things which really makes life in this business worthwhile."

Liebendorfer wrote Cavagnaro that "I hope you have read Mr. Newman's book, 'The Impact of Southern Football'. I not only read it, I felt it."

On March 2, Liebendorfer wrote to Zipp with professional and personal affinity:

"Thank you very much for sending me the wonderful presentation on the State of Alabama Sports Hall of Fame Induction Dinner. This is a beautiful job as in any other project with which you are associated. That must have been a great evening, and I'm sure one that none of you ever will forget.

My congratulations to all of you and very best wishes for continued success ... and especially my thanks to you personally for never forgetting me."[5]

His letter of March 4, 1970 thanked Zipp for sending a tear sheet of a tribute to Hank Crisp.[6] Crisp died January 23, 1970 in Birmingham.

Liebendorfer published a book in 1972 titled *The Color of Life Is Red: A History of Stanford Athletics 1892-1972*. The 331-page book is a compilation of histories of Stanford University's founder, administrators, coaches, players and their achievements.

In 1920 Liebendorfer entered Stanford University as a freshman. Born in New Brighton, Pennsylvania, he grew up in Modesto, California.[7] He and Zipp had a long professional relationship which developed into a wonderful personal relationship as testified in his line above: "my thanks to you for personally never forgetting me."

Hall of Fame Nomination

Tom Willingham, who considered himself a football buff, on February 25, 1970, wrote Zipp a three-fold purpose letter. He wished to nominate two men to the Alabama Sports Hall of Fame; to make a request to Zipp; and to send a list to Zipp.

Since the inaugural ASHOF had now passed, Willingham wished to secure two future nominations, knowing the influence Newman possessed regarding nominations and also knowing that Newman was, to say the least, a modest man.[8]

Willingham put forth the name of a former Decatur [Alabama] High School football coach, H.L. "Shorty" Ogle. ("Shorty" was 6 feet 4.) He coached four undefeated State Championship teams, beginning his first year of 1933. In 1979 Ogle was inducted into the Alabama Sports Hall of Fame, the first high school coach to be so honored.[9]

The other nomination by Willingham actually came first in his letter.

> "The first man I want to nominate is Mr. Henry H. "Zipp" Newman, a man whose love for sports and his great talent in writing of sports sets him apart from ordinary people."

Newman's day would come.

Willingham's request concerned the 1955, all-time teams from each SEC school that Zipp created. Given that fifteen years had passed, and many of those players had performed well, presumably professionally, Willingham wrote,

> "Therefore, I ask that you select these teams again. Please, this is a sports service that only you can do."

Lastly, he thought that Zipp might be interested in "a copy of my all-Southeastern Conference team for the 1960s."

Raymond Johnson, months before retiring from his sportswriting profession, wrote to Zipp on February 26, 1970 about the very fine *Tennessee Sports Hall of Fame* dinner on February 20. Johnson for many years was sportswriter and editor of *The* [Nashville] *Tennessean* newspaper.[10] He was considered an expert on the "Sport of Kings" and covered many Kentucky Derby races. Both Johnson and Newman loved horse racing. Apparently, based on his letter writing and articles, Johnson had a gregarious quality to his character.

This letter to Newman was typed on plain paper – "please pardon this fancy stationery," opened Johnson. He apologized to Zipp for missing the *Alabama Sports Hall of Fame* induction dinner as he had previously planned. He told Zipp he was clearing out his desk for John Bibb who would be replacing him as sports editor.

> "I ran across a Southern League Baseball Writers Association card of 1931. Guess who signed it? None other than Zipp Newman."

The almost retired Johnson told Zipp that before March 31 – his official retirement date – he would be covering the Triple Crown races in Kentucky, Maryland, and New York, then on to the South for the Flamingo and Florida derbies. He closed this letter telling Zipp that he was available for fishing, hunting, golf anytime.[11]

In early May, Johnson and Newman talked on the telephone. Johnson followed up that conversation in a letter saying,

> "After our conversation the other night, you probably think I am nuts for asking you to put in writing the answers to a number of questions. The reason is that the Tennessee Sports Hall of Fame wants me to become its executive secretary. I want to know more about it before the mule is loaded down with more than he can pull. Hence the questions.[12]

Johnson put forward a litany of questions, including: What's the difference between being a consultant and an executive secretary; Does Zipp handle most of the ASHOF letter writing and paperwork; Does Zipp have a secretary or stenographer? The questions were numerous and on one page. Raymond Johnson's questions made it clear that he wanted to know from the expert to what extent the workload entailed. He then switched topics.

He wrote about changing the dates of the Tennessee Sports Hall of Fame induction ceremony in future years and hoping to attract notable people. He closed this May 9, 1970 letter with,

> "I would be most grateful if you will supply these answers within the next couple of weeks. I'm going to Louisville Monday to meet with Churchill Downs officials on some problems Turf Writers have. Also will meet with motel folks. Then head to Baltimore for the Preakness on Saturday. Gratefully, Raymond."

The 1970s

Two weeks was not a lot of time for Zipp to reply. But he did. Although grateful for the two brochures and Zipp's accompanying letter which supplied a lot of answers, Johnson answered with a zinger in his reply to Zipp on May 23:

> "To be honest with you, I DO NOT want this job."

Johnson acknowledged that he had a lot of "other irons in the fire." And the job did not pay well. He noted that he was a director of the Amateur Softball Association of America, was president of it between 1942 and 1948, and he was named president of the National Turf Writers Association in April 1970.

Johnson, however, wanted to be helpful.

> "Don't misunderstand me: I want to do anything I can to help promote what I feel is a good thing and the Tennessee Sports Hall of Fame [could] be a good thing if properly handled."[13]

By August, Raymond Johnson was the director of publicity at Churchill Downs. On Churchill Downs stationery he wrote to Zipp, while in Knoxville, that a dozen or so sportswriters who had covered Tennessee football would be honored on September 16 at a luncheon and then again at the night football game.

> "I sincerely hope that you and your wife can make it. ... Now, what I am attempting to say is that we [Raymond and wife Mae] would be delighted to have you and your wife accompany us from Knoxville to Louisville to Nashville. I would like to show you ... Churchill Downs as few people get to see it."[14]

Zipp replied, then Johnson wrote him again from Memphis on the hotel stationery where he was lodged, saying:

> "Dear Zipp: Many thanks for your prompt reply, which caught up with me here yesterday. I don't recall whether I told you but I was chosen to represent the Baseball Writers Association of America at the American Legion's World Series which opened here [Memphis] Thursday morning and continues through Tuesday night. ... We are sorry to hear the bad news about your wife. We hope the special shots

are helping her ear trouble and high blood pressure. We had sincerely hoped that you and Frances could make it to Knoxville and go on to Louisville with us. You have a rain check anytime you want to use it. ..."[15]

So much for Johnson's retirement.

Helms Athletic Foundation

W.R. "Bill" Schroeder, Managing Director, Helms Athletic Foundation – Helms Hall, wrote to Newman on March 2, 1970. Zipp mailed him a note and clipping for which Schroeder thanked him. Schroeder attached to his letter a listing of the Southeastern Conference Players who had been cited for Helms All-America team honors in the past.[16]

Zipp Newman was always on the list of certain sports associations as a contributor to sports-newsworthy items such as "the best-ever college football team of the 1930s." By the 1970s Zipp had been around a long time in the sports world, and he knew virtually every major sports enthusiast in the nation – one was William R. "Bill" Schroeder.

Schroeder and Paul Helms together founded the Helms Athletic Foundation in 1936 in Los Angeles, California. Helms owned a bakery operation in New York but retired at age thirty-seven because of ill health. Two years later in 1938, Helms, not one to be idle, moved with his family to Los Angeles to "re-start" his bakery business, which became a huge financial success.

How Schroeder and Helms got together is not known, but they teamed to organize the Helms Athletic Foundation. According to some sources, the Foundation was not a foundation at all because it had no sustaining financial support. It was mis-named. The "Foundation" was funded by Helms's bakery operations.

Both Helms and Schroeder loved sports and began to name or to identify national champions in various sports, going back to 1883 for football, and in basketball from 1900 to 1942. It was Schroeder who actually determined, then named champions. This was an example of two men taking the initiative to start something. It was arbitrary, requiring no authentication from a third party. Over the years the Helms organization, its athletic selections, and its accumulation of sports artifacts, provided a legitimacy and/or authentication for its efforts.

The 1970s

This March 2, 1970 letter from Bill Schroeder to Zipp, and all other letters to Zipp, had the salutation "Dear Friend Zipp." That alone tells the reader that a wonderful business and personal relationship thrived between the two men. Also, Zipp and Bill were past their prime working careers, but neither knew it, or they carried on as if they were forty years younger.

Schroeder, acknowledging that he now knew who was planning to select an all-time Southeastern Conference Basketball Team, attached a listing of all the SEC Conference players "who had been cited for the Helms Athletic Foundation College Basketball Team honors in the past."

Schroeder wrote that the Helms Athletic Foundation would not make its 1970 selections until after the National Championship Tournament in March. He also assured Zipp that he would honor his commitment to the Alabama Sports Hall of Fame with a plaque bearing all the names of the Alabama greats "who have been cited by our Foundation."

Zipp wrote to Schroeder on July 12 that he wished to receive photos of Helms Hall and Schroeder himself. Schroeder returned in a letter of July 17 to Zipp saying that he was surprised that Zipp had not yet received the photos. He also mentioned that he hoped it would be possible for him to make the trip to Birmingham for the USC-Alabama football game in the fall. [17] There was lag time between letters and mail delivery.

On the next day, July 17, Schroeder wrote that he

> "was pleased to receive your note ... in which you enlightened that you received the photographs which I sent to you."

Newman did not know that Deke Houlgate wrote the *Football Thesaurus* [in 1946]. Schroeder wrote that he would mail copies of that book under separate cover, "for I know that Deke would have very much wanted you to have the book."[18]

Word gets around. Schroeder wrote on July 30,

> "I was delighted to learn that your Hall of Fame Committee has extended an invitation to Braven Dyer, with all expenses paid, to attend the Alabama-USC Football game, and all of the ceremonies which will be held in connection with it. Braven, of course, will be a superb ambassador for Southern California."

Braven Dyer wrote to Zipp, but it is not certain whether or not Schroeder was aware – unless Dyer told him. But since both Dyer and Schroeder were West Coast people, they talked. Dyer's letter to Zipp provided information about his efforts to get himself to the USC-Alabama game.

> "Ever since the game was announced I have been trying to put together a chartered flight for the Alabama-USC meeting in Tuscaloosa next September. It has been rather low, most because people of my age are rather reluctant to sign up and kick in their money at this time." [19]

There is no question that Newman was the instrumental agent getting the "all expenses paid" trip for Braven Dyer from Los Angeles to Birmingham. Everyone knew that the match-up between the two schools was more than just football.

Closing his letter to Zipp, Bill Schroeder sounded somewhat like Braven Dyer:

> "I rather doubt if I shall be able to travel to Birmingham for the Alabama-USC Football game – unless TWA might be taking some of the Southern California boosters to Birmingham, via charter.
>
> As you know, I am the Sports Consultant for TWA, and it is by this plane travel that I am able to make trips abroad and travel around the country." [20]

Dwight Keith wrote to Zipp asking him for any statistical information he had on Georgia Tech football star Joe Guyon. [21] Keith had requested the same from George Griffin, a long time "patriot" of Georgia Tech.

Griffin was known as "Mr. Georgia Tech" and possessor of his own sports collection of Georgia Tech history. Keith said that Griffin considered Joe Guyon was the best all-around football player there and that Coach [W.A.] Alexander told him that he saw Guyon jump the five-foot picket fence around Grant Field in full football uniform "with ease." As interesting as that was, what Keith wrote in the second paragraph was quite unusual.

"I wish I could remember the details but Coach Alex also told me about Guyon leaving school to find someone who had killed a relative of his. He finally found him somewhere far out West, got his revenge and returned to school."

Guyon, a Chippewa Indian born in 1892 in Minnesota, compiled impressive statistics as a football athlete, not only at Georgia Tech but in professional football. Inducted into the Pro Football Hall of Fame in 1966, he entered the College Football Hall of Fame in 1971. He played minor league baseball and later coached baseball at Clemson University.

Before playing football at Georgia Tech, Guyon played at the Carlisle Indian School from 1912 to 1913, and then at the Keewatin Academy in Wisconsin. His years at Georgia Tech were 1917 and 1918. His time at Keewatin was to regain college eligibility.[22] There is no record outside of Keith's letter, verifying "Guyon's revenge."

William Heymans, Secretary-Treasurer of the Chicago Cubs, acknowledged receipt of Zipp's article addressed to Mr. Philip K. Wrigley. This response dated May 15, 1970, closed with,

"We wish to thank you for sending along your very nice article and for your long support of the Cubs."[23]

This short letter makes clear two things – that Zipp wrote about the activities of the Cubs' team and its players, and that Zipp had a working relationship with the organization.

Zipp Newman turned 76 years old on May 24, 1970. Ten days later he heard from his friend at Auburn. Wilbur Hutsell wrote,

"Dear Henry:

Thanks a heap for your kind words. Mighty sorry you could not be here for 'A' Day – cause Corinne and I thoroughly enjoyed it.

I am organizing a 'woods' warming, as so many trees are on the site of the new track – everybody to bring an axe.

Your article on Howard Hill was fine – have mailed a copy to his old team mate Charlie Dudley in Columbus, Georgia."[24]

Auburn University was in the process of expanding its sports environment by constructing new athletic and office buildings and outdoor venues. It was an exciting time for Hutsell and he always shared his enthusiasm for Auburn's "goings on" with Zipp.

On Sunday July 19, 1970 Zipp published an article in *The Birmingham News* about Alabama's All-time Major League Club. Virgil Lawrence "Spud" Davis was a major league baseball player. He was born in Birmingham and was catcher for the St. Louis Cardinals, Philadelphia Phillies, Cincinnati Reds, and the Pittsburgh Pirates.

Spud Davis wrote briefly to Zipp after reading the article.

> "Just a note to thank you for your kind recognition in last Sunday's article ... I enjoy your articles and always look forward to 'Dusting 'Em Off.'" [25]

USC-Alabama

The University of Southern California played the University of Alabama in the season's opening game on September 12, 1970 at Legion Field in Birmingham. Alabama lost 42-21. Alabama continued its season while losing five games, including the Iron Bowl with Auburn. Alabama tied Houston in the Astro Bluebonnet Bowl on December 31, 1970. But it was that season opening game that made history.

The build-up to the game pitted two college football powerhouses dueling for the right to claim themselves the best. Sportswriters from across the nation wanted to cover this particular game. Braven Dyer of the *Los Angeles Times* and Bill Schroeder of the Helms Athletic Foundation. How did the game come about?

Certainly, Zipp Newman knew Alabama head coach Paul "Bear" Bryant. And there might have been some exchange at that time between the two about the game's origin. The southernmost football teams in the Southeastern Conference were composed of all white players. Southern California's football team was integrated, with an African American quarterback.

Secret Meeting

Coach Bryant met with USC coach John McKay one day at LAX airport in Los Angeles. Bryant had asked for the meeting. Simply put, Bryant asked McKay to bring his USC team to Birmingham to play Alabama in the opening game.

McKay asked, and Bryant replied, that they would pay USC $150,000. McKay then said that if Alabama played USC in Los Angeles the following year, he would pay $250,000. But this is still not the real story.

Coach Bryant wanted to recruit African American football players, but he could not, because of who sat in the Governor's mansion in Montgomery and the climate of the times. Bringing USC to Birmingham might just begin to break the segregation barrier. And, it did.

We will not go into this story any deeper, because that one game has been documented extensively. But one wonders whether Braven Dyer and Bill Schroeder and their wanting to be present at the game knew of the game's undertone.

Two weeks later the Auburn-Tennessee football game was played at Legion Field in Birmingham. Auburn defeated #17 Tennessee 36-33.

The chief talent scout for the then-named Boston Patriots Football Club, Ed McKeever, attended the Auburn-Tennessee game in Birmingham. Two days later, after returning to Boston, he wrote,

> "Dear Zipp: THANKS A MILLION for your nice comments when I attended the Tennessee-Auburn game in Birmingham. My daughter, who lives in Pensacola, sent me the article – which only means, as you so well know, your WRITING covers a wide area. ... Hope everything is going well with you Zipp. Gratefully, Ed."[26]

On September 28 Michael C. Matsos copied Zipp on his letter to Thomas Hamilton of the Pacific-8 Conference in San Francisco, writing that Zipp gave Matsos a copy of

> "[Y]our September 22 letter and your distinguished picture ... Your efforts to secure the photograph of the Rose Bowl Stadium and the Southeastern Conference Teams that have participated in the Rose Bowl will be most appreciated."[27]

Frances Newman Morris

Matsos, a restaurateur and the proprietor of Michael's Enterprises on South 20th Street in Birmingham, was visited sometime earlier by Thomas Hamilton and noted that the two "had such limited time ... we did not have an opportunity to really show you around." He invited him to visit again next time he was in Birmingham. Zipp was central in getting the exchange of photos and other memorabilia.

Ed Leigh McMillan was chairman of the T.R. Miller Mill Company in Brewton, Alabama. Zipp wrote to him on October 28, 1970 with tickets to the annual Thanksgiving Day Crippled Children's Clinic football game.

> "Dear Zipp, I have your letter containing two tickets ... I am returning the tickets to you, you can give them to some worthy person. I am enclosing a check for $100.00 payable to the Crippled Children's Clinic."[28]

The letter then became personal and the retired eighty-two-year-old former turkey hunter updated Zipp on his personal life.

The Crippled Children's Clinic High School Football Game was played on Thanksgiving Day, November 26, 1970 in Birmingham. Ramsey High School defeated 31-22 Ensley High School.[29]

1971 Letters

Sports fans become excited when one of their favorite athletes – or friends – makes it into a hall of fame. Many express their excitement by writing a letter to or calling the athlete so elected. Some people know whom to thank.

Walter R. Bogart, Jr. wrote to Zipp on January 9, 1971 that he was recently in his hometown of Stevenson, Alabama during the Christmas holiday and became elated over the news that Sanders Russell would be inducted into the Alabama Sports Hall of Fame later in the month.[30]

> "This is certainly wonderful, and I am deeply grateful to you for everything you did in behalf of Mr. Russell ... My very best to you and yours for a most rewarding 1971."

C.H. Pearson of the Pearson Advertising Agency, Inc., NYC. sent a letter to Zipp dated January 27, 1971.

"Mr. Newman, In connection with our Football Book, COLLEGE FOOTBALL U.S.A., which will be the official book for the National Football Foundation and Hall of Fame, I would very much appreciate your permission to reprint your article on The Modern Football Team."

Bert McGrane, who for many years was secretary-treasurer of The Football Writers Association of America, sent materials to Pearson with his permission to reprint the Early Day and Modern All Time Teams for inclusion into the planned football book. Additionally, McGrane included a copy of Newman's article "The Modern Football Team." Pearson liked the article so much that he sought permission directly from Zipp to reprint the article. [31]

Lloyd Gregory, Lloyd Gregory & Associates, Houston, Texas wrote on February 9, 1971:

"Dear Zipp, Our mutual friend, Morris Frank, sent me a copy of your column which I found very interesting. It seems only yesterday that the Birmingham Barons and the Houston Buffs [Buffaloes] were playing in the 1928 Dixie [minor league baseball] Series. P.S. Morris yesterday was named president of the Bluebonnet Bowl." [32]

Frank Wallace of the International Sports and Games Research Collection at the Memorial Library of the University of Notre Dame wrote on April 30:

"Dear Zipp: Thank you very much for your note. I am writing this [letter] from the Library at Notre Dame. We shall have more mail coming your way which will give you a better picture of what we are trying to do.

In the meantime, if you have any letters, records, or other memorabilia, we would very much like to add it to our Collection ...

We hope to bring in as many people as yourself as possible, who will make this Collection the first institution of its kind, and emphasize

The 1970s

the importance of all sports, amateur and professional, on the American culture."[33]

The traffic of sports artifacts was a two-way street. Zipp Newman offered memorabilia when asked, and he donated to institutions also, when not necessarily asked.

A Notre Dame graduate, Roger Kiley, was a Judge on the Seventh Circuit, United States Court of Appeals, Chicago. He was an All-America football player at the University of Notre Dame. He wrote on June 1, 1971:

> "Dear Zipp: Porter Grant sent me the Birmingham News sports sheet, all about Auburn, and I came across your column, with pictures of, among others, my old friend Tommy [no surname written]. This was a happy turn of events and revived many memories of days long ago. Best wishes for good health. And I hope that all the predictions about Auburn next fall come true." [34]

The Notre Dame football team of 1919 went undefeated. Kiley and the infamous George Gipp played under legendary coach Knute Rockne. The school's post-season review of the team and each coach and player said that,

> "When Kiley found that the "Aerial Twins," Kirk and E. Anderson, were competing with him for the position of end, he did not lose hope of becoming a regular but only fought the harder, and as a result he emerges from the season a monogram man. "Rog" did his share of retrieving forward passes and also became known and feared as one of the hardest and surest tacklers on the team. Few gains were made around his flank and fewer still are the men who managed to shake him off once he had them. With Kiley back for next year, and the year after, the important position of end ceases to be a problem for the coaches."[35]

Tram Sessions wrote a letter on June 16, 1971 after Zipp Newman visited with him and others. Zipp was on a fund-raising mission.

> "Hi Zip [sic]: Was swell of you and Dick [no surname written] to come by and see me. I am fine now. We had a meeting of the Board Tuesday, everybody here was there but Alex Lacy & Paul Crisp, both

being out of town. Jess Lanier is a good worker and close as he is to Frank House we really gained another good guy. Sorry we have no money. You know the banquet broke us. We only have about $800.00 to run to Sept. or really 1st of October. Come by to see me."[36]

Sessions played center for the Alabama Crimson Tide football team and was the first secretary-treasurer of the Alabama Sports Hall of Fame as Zipp was the organization's first executive secretary. In 1945 he sponsored a bill to renew/revive the Alabama-Auburn football rivalry.[37]

Roy B. Sewell, of the Sewell Manufacturing Company in Bremen, Georgia wrote:

"Dear Zipp: Thank you for your nice write-up you gave me in your column on June 30 [1971] – I appreciate your kind remarks. It was wonderful seeing you and Dick [no surname written]. If possible – let's be better friends every day."[38]

Wilbur (W.H.) Hutsell at Auburn University penned a letter on Labor Day:

"Dear Zipp [and not 'Dear Henry']:

Train rides for football travel discussed in yesterday's [September 5, 1971] column were most interesting. The coaches and sportswriters of the era were close friends, and trips to the games were wonderful memories.

You and I probably set a mileage record for Gin Rummy on the trip to West Point. Jack Meagher's stops for practice going to and from the Santa game can't be forgotten either, including an entire day in Los Angeles."[39]

Meagher was head football coach at Auburn University from 1934 to 1942. His assistant coach was Ralph "Shug" Jordan [pronounced jer-dun]. Amazingly, in Meagher's first six years coaching at Auburn all but three games were played at home. His coaching strategy was aggressiveness, and his former players at Auburn were known as "Meagher's Marauders."[40]

Zipp Newman and his family were Episcopalians and members of the Church of the Advent in downtown Birmingham. The Reverend Charles Clingman was the third rector of that parish. He and Zipp Newman became close friends. Clingman after several years serving at the Advent was elected bishop of the Episcopal Diocese of Louisville, causing him to leave Birmingham.

Robert Jemison, Jr., a friend of Zipp and president of a Birmingham real estate firm bearing his surname, wrote to Zipp on November 16, 1971:

> "Dear Zipp: I understand that the announcement of the death of Bishop Clingman in Louisville [Kentucky] last week was made at the morning Service – at the Church of the Advent. I am sorry that the information was not given to the Press, as Bishop Clingman was a much beloved and useful Rector at the Church of the Advent for more than ten years, before his removal to Louisville, Ky., to become bishop. As I know you are a personal friend of Bishop Clingman I hope that some mention can be made in the Press about his death ..."[41]

Jemison told Zipp that Clingman's death was also a personal loss to him.

1972 Letters
Dwight Keith sold his *Coach and Athlete* magazine in 1972.[42]

Zipp wrote to Gabriel Paul, president of the Cleveland Indians Baseball organization, asking him for any and all information he might have on Satchel Paige. Paul replied:

> "Dear Zipp: I am asking my publicity department to send you whatever they have on Satchel Paige for his induction into the Alabama Sports Hall of Fame on January 14."

Paul continued:

> "I do miss the good times we used to have and I want to tell you what a bang I got out of hearing from you." [43]

This correspondence between Zipp Newman and Gabriel Paul is another example of the personal and professional relationships Zipp developed over the decades.

In Newman's *Dusting 'Em Off* column of February 20, 1972 headlined *"Yellowsally Jeff back at desk and yearning to fish,"* Zipp told his readers about a friend who had recently recovered from surgery after spending two full weeks in Tuscaloosa's Druid City Hospital.

Zipp called Coleman to check on him – "I'm feeling fine" – and then asked Zipp "When are we going fishing at Dollarhide." Jefferson Coleman would have to take it easy for a while and miss his annual quail hunt outing.

Coleman was Wallace Wade's secretary when Wade coached the Crimson Tide football team. Zipp wrote that

> "Since Jeff watched the first Alabama Rose Bowl game on Jan. 1, 1926, he has seen more Alabama games than any other Tide follower." [44]

Later, on March 22, 1972 Coleman wrote a letter to Zipp saying,

> "Dear Zipp: I enjoyed reading about your recent visit to Dollarhide. Nine of us tried to find a turkey on opening day. Joe Sewell saw one gobbler and five hens but none of us were able to get up on a gobbler close enough." [45]

Coleman wanted to know the dates Zipp had planned for his upcoming fishing activities at Dollarhide. He was concerned about invited fishing contestants and how he would get them to Dollarhide.

> "Be thinking about the dates and you might want to check with some of your invitees and see when they might be available."

Coleman said that from that point forward he would leave everything else in Zipp's hands. But he didn't.

On April 24, 1972 Jeff Coleman mailed invitations that read:

"[Invitee Name – handwritten]
YOU ARE CORDIALLY INVITED:

To Attend the
ZIPP NEWMAN FISHING FESTIVAL
(Strictly not a contest or rodeo)
All mentioned in the enclosed <u>Dusting 'Em Off</u> are
cordially invited to join us at Dollarhide for <u>all</u> or <u>part</u>
of the time shown below.

May 17, Wednesday afternoon fishing
May 18, Thursday All day fishing
May 19, Friday (Break camp after lunch)

We guarantee to put you on bass – or bream. All
you need bring is your tackle and toothbrush.
Should you need information on travel – how to reach
Dollarhide – just let me know and details will be sent
immediately.
I hope you can be with us.
P.S.
<u>This is not for publication</u>
<u>until after the fact. Suggest</u>
<u>you keep these dates confidential</u>
<u>except for your own personal purposes.</u>

RSVP: Enclosed is post paid envelop for
your convenience in letting me know when
you will arrive and how long you will stay,
or in what part of the schedule listed above
you will participate.[46]

In May Coleman wrote a memo-like letter to Zipp, Alf Van Hoose and Boyd Aman, with a copy to Mr. Sam H. Wright.

"Enclosed you will find a few more worms from Sam Wright of Sylacauga [Alabama]. These [worms] are from the Dallas F. Weldon Bait Company ...

The 1970s

These are made by the same company as the worm I gave you at Dollarhide. Sam Wright sends these to you with his best wishes."[47]

On March 30, 1972, (Mrs.) Eloise Metzger Cooper wrote a letter of gratitude to Newman.

"Dear Mr. Newman:

The enclosed Xerox copy of The Atlanta Journal and Constitution on Sunday, July 27, 1969, was so exciting to mother (Mrs. William E. Metzger) and all the children and grandchildren. It is wonderful to know that after all these years Daddy is still remembered as the great player he was ..."[48]

Tony Ulrich, custodian and director of the *Dick Lamb Football Collection at the Football Information Bureau*, mailed an announcement to Zipp Newman and other sportswriters of the relocation of the Bureau, due to the death of Richard "Dick" Lamb.

"The entire Dick Lamb collection of football historical material is now under my custodianship and direction and is the largest private collection of this kind."

Ulrich handwrote on Zipp's copy of his general announcement mailed to more than 475 colleges. He assured readers of the announcement that the Bureau would continue to provide historical and statistical data to those seeking such information.[49]

Ten days later on April 25 Ulrich handwrote a letter to Zipp.

"Dear Mr. Newman: It was wonderful talking with you the other night. You know, I'm going to hold you to your fine invitation to the Alabama game and the Governor's dinner the night before. Is it a black-tie affair?

With this letter I am enclosing some background information about the Bureau and (blush) myself.

I take it you met Dick Lamb somewhere in your journeys about this land. He was a prince of a fellow. Hope to hear from you soon."[50]

Three weeks later Ulrich handwrote another letter.

> "Dear Zipp. It seems like I write or phone you most every-other-day.
> I hope you have received the book "Oh, How They Played the Game."
>
> I have a nice letter from the manager – Mr. Tom Kelly – of the
> Parliament House [hotel in Birmingham] requesting my
> reservations. I take it – that is the best place in town and most
> certainly OK with me. I will write to him in a day or two. Many
> thanks, Tony."[51]

In yet another handwritten note, this one of August 26, Ulrich wrote,

> "Dear Zipp: Just a quickie. ..." Writes about the book he suggested
> earlier "A History of Southern Football, 1890-1928" by Fuzzy
> Woodruff. The oddity in 1917 was that Georgia Tech played a double-
> header on September 29. They beat Furman and Wake Forest. In 1926
> Navy beat Drake and Richmond. Ulrich wrote that he finished reading
> Impact.[52]

Ulrich traveled from Dayton to Birmingham and stayed at the *Parliament
Hotel* in October. Overwhelmed by how he was treated, he typed a letter
to Zipp saying,

> "Dear Zipp: THANKS. I have heard of Southern hospitality but never
> savored its meaning. Birmingham has it in spades. As dose [sic] Zipp
> Newman. As I think back on those wonderful days I can remember
> the first lunch that was truly Oriental and dam [sic] good. Then the
> civic lunch wher [sic] Fred Sington announced me to those attending.
>
> ... Also, I heed your words about the movement of the game's
> influence from the East to other sections of the nation. ..."[53]

The year 1972 for Tony Ulrich ended with a wonderful Christmas Eve
handwritten letter.

> "Dear Zipp: I want to thank you for your wonderful Christmas card
> and the words you inscribed thereon.

My association with you (and Dick) is something I think about every day. As I write this football book I keep thinking – Would Zipp like it? or Would Zipp say it this way? I am so much an amateur at this sort of thing. But I strive to improve.

Zipp, you have no way of knowing what (or how) our conversations have broadened my scope of thinking. ..."[54]

The annual Goose Dinner event, sponsored by Mr. Cecil Wood, was held in Scottsboro, Alabama on June 8, 1972. The next day Floyd H. Mann, Special Assistant to the President of The University of Alabama wrote:

"Dear Mr. Newman: I enjoyed getting to see you in Scottsboro yesterday, and I was so pleased that this entire meeting seem [sic] to involve around the tremendous contributions that you have made to this State over a long period of time. I was indeed pleased that they gave you a tribute to such a fine citizen. I wish sometime when you are in Tuscaloosa you will drop by for a visit."[55]

Richard Thigpen, the Executive Assistant to the President of The University of Alabama, also attended the Goose Dinner. He wrote,

"Dear Mr. Newman: It was a pleasure to visit briefly with you at the annual goose dinner ... Needless to say, we at The University of Alabama take great pride in participating in this annual occasion, since, as Mr. Cavaleri indicated, it has its origin in an effort by yourself and others to raise funds for our crippled children's clinic program in Birmingham."[56]

Southeastern Conference Commissioner Tonto Coleman, wrote to Zipp on July 5, 1972,

"Dear Zipp: I appreciate so much the kind things you had to say about me in Sunday's paper. I think I've never known a sportswriter who did so much for so many."[57]

C.H. Pearson of the Pearson Advertising Agency wrote on July 11,

"Dear Mr. Newman: Thank you for your fine letter of June 12th. Also, that magnificent article that appeared in the June 25th issue of the

Birmingham News is very kind. You were very kind. Should you happen to have a close friend who would like a complimentary copy of COLLEGE FOOTBALL U.S.A., please let me know and I will see to it that he gets it promptly."

Zipp, in return provided the name of Ted Kakoliris and his address.[58] Kakoliris, a native of Birmingham, was a third-baseman for four minor league teams. His first two seasons were with the Lincoln [Nebraska] Links in 1938 and 1939, affiliated with the St. Louis Browns. After that he played within the St. Louis Cardinals system: first with Pocatello [Idaho] Cardinals and the Decatur [Illinois] Commodores in 1940; returned to Pocatello in 1941. In 1946 he played for the Lynchburg Cardinals.[59]

In late July the Director of the Birmingham Park & Recreation Center, Frank A. Wagner, wrote:

"Dear Zipp: Just a note to thank you for your nice article you wrote about me in last Sunday's paper. Although it was not all true, I appreciate the nice things you said."[60]

George R. Woodruff, Athletic Director, University of Tennessee sent Zipp an invitation to attend their honor ceremonies and then the first night football game of the 1972 season.

"Dear Zipp:

The University of Tennessee Athletic Department will be pleased to have you and your wife as honored guests at the 1972 Press Party for the "First Nighter" football game, U.T. vs. Penn State, to be held at 12 o'clock noon, September 16, at the Hyatt Regency House. We plan to honor members of the Press who have covered Volunteer football for 25 years or longer."[61]

This invitation is what Raymond Johnson alluded to in an earlier letter to Zipp. The luncheon tribute of September 16, 1972 in Knoxville drew seven hundred Tennessee football supporters. Zipp and wife Frances were not present.

The Chancellor of The University of Tennessee, Archie R. Dykes, wrote on September 19,

The 1970s

"Dear Zipp: We regret that you were unable to be with us Saturday for the luncheon in honor of you and your colleagues who have covered athletic events at The University of Tennessee, Knoxville for the past quarter century ...

"We especially appreciate the consistently fair and objective coverage you have given The University of Tennessee athletic teams. We hope our programs will continue to merit your interest and support."[62]

Robert B. Scheffing, Vice President & General Manager of the New York National League Baseball Club responded on August 8, 1972 to an inquiry from Newman.

"Dear Mr. Newman: We do not request Casey Stengel to go to any events for us, outside of our own Old Timer's game here in New York, and the Baseball Writer's annual dinner. Casey does make some appearances, and I suggest you write to him at [Stengel's address provided here].[63]

Elbert S. Jemison, Jr., was President & Treasurer of Jemison Securities Corporation in Birmingham. In August of 1972 he wrote:

"Dear Zipp: This is in connection with your phone call to me yesterday. I believe the best place to start in locating pictures of the ten leading money winners for either 1971 or 1972 would be the Tournament Players Division of the Professional Golf Association."[64]

Paul M. Grist of Selma, Alabama wrote to Zipp to make a nomination.

"Dear Zipp: ... I would like to submit the name of Mr. William Gray Little as a candidate for the Alabama Sports Hall of Fame. ..."[65]

Letters of nomination to the Alabama Sports Hall of Fame addressed to Zipp were not unusual. Newman held great influence in his later years due to his continued activities writing about the sports world. In this case Mr. Grist noted that William Gray Little was the subject of a column Zipp wrote about this "Father of Football" at the University of Alabama. To assist Zipp with any further information Grist provided the name and address of Coach Little's daughter, who maintained a scrapbook of her father's football days.

Ken Smith, Director of the National Baseball Hall of Fame and Museum, Inc. wrote to Zipp on November 1, 1972 thanking him for his recent letter.

> "Hope the Birmingham Southern League franchise gets set up properly, it has a rich background, if only the younger generation could finally get it into its head what a direct tie-up there is between the local team and the ones they see on the screen. ..."[66]

He also mentions in his letter Mike Barlow, Phil Cavarretta, Hal Totten, Billy Hitchcock. This is just one letter depicting how "old timers" reinforce their memories of people and good times. The letters begin with mostly "business" and close with words like "Do you remember?"

Bob Shepherd of Shepherd Realty Company, Inc. Birmingham thanked Zipp for an article about his Dad.

> "Your column is always so full of memories which always has such feeling to so many people. Dad always cherished your friendship for the many years you have known each other."[67]

The letter was dated November 28, 1972.

1973 Letters
On February 7, 1973 Sammy Barnes of Louisville, Mississippi wrote,

> "Dear Zipp: Under separate cover I have mailed to you at the Birmingham News Office my description of the fight between Billy Evans and Ty Cobb. ...
>
> "I enclosed a negative, which if you see fit to use or not, I'd appreciate it eventually being returned to me ... I tried to give you my version of the 'Baseball Battle of the Century.'"[68]

The 1973 Induction Ceremony and Dinner of the Alabama Sports Hall of Fame took place on February 16.

The Associate Rector of The Church of the Nativity in Huntsville, Alabama gave the invocation.

> *Dear God, we thank you for your gifts of life and love. We thank you for times of work and play, of labor and rest. We thank you for the disciplines of body, mind, and spirit; for the joy and satisfaction of making full use of your gifts.*
>
> *We thank you, Lord, for sports – for the fun of playing and watching them, for the lifelong habits of discipline, fairness, and loyalty which we learn through them, for the fortitude we develop through them which helps us to stand in adversity as well as in prosperity.*
>
> *We thank you, Lord, for those whose achievements, in sports and in all of life, have delighted and inspired us, and held before us a vision of human potential. In honoring them we honor your gifts, and we honor ourselves.*
>
> *Father, as we eat and drink together and honor your children, we celebrate your presence among us and within us. Yours is the kingdom and the power and the glory, now and forever. Amen.* [69]

The Associate Rector who gave the Invocation was Hoyt Winslett, Jr. His father, Hoyt "Wu" Winslett, a University of Alabama, all around football great who played under Coach Wallace Wade, played in the two Rose Bowl games of 1926 and 1927. "Wu" Winslett was inducted into the Alabama Sports Hall of Fame that evening.

"Wu" Winslett, who was at that time president of Dollarhide Camp, Inc., penned a handwritten letter to Zipp.

> "Now that the smoke has all cleared away, let me thank you once again for all the interest you have taken in me over the years. And a special thanks for your help in getting me in the Hall of Fame! My family joins me in all this.
>
> "Let's get down to fishing now and I look forward to seeing you at Dollarhide." [70]

Wilbur Hutsell's wife Corinne died on January 27, 1973. Three weeks later Hutsell wrote to Zipp.

"Dear Zipp: Corinne's death was a dreadful shock, although it was not unexpected ...

"The letter from Frances and you was most comforting. Your friendship is the Senior one in my recollection, as it will have covered 54 years next August, with never a doubtful moment."[71]

Richard Thigpen, Executive Assistant to the President of the University of Alabama, wrote to Mr. Cecil B. Word and copied to Zipp Newman and Colonel Floyd Mann.

"It was a pleasure to visit briefly with you at the recent Hall of Fame Dinner in Birmingham. I since received your note of February 26, and all of us are looking forward to your [Goose] dinner [in Scottsboro] on April 24. ..."[72]

Luke Sewell was one of three brothers from Alabama who played professional baseball. On March 2, 1972, J. Luther Sewell wrote,

"Dear Zipp: It was a genuine pleasure seeing you while in Birmingham and want you to know I feel greatly indebted to you for being inducted into the Alabama Sports Hall of Fame as it was you who nominated me ..."[73]

John W. Boebinger, President of the New Orleans Mid-Winter Sports Association [Sugar Bowl], sent an air mail letter to Zipp dated May 22, 1973.

"Dear Zipp: All of the Sugar Bowlers and Edna Engert join with me at the time to extend a happy birthday wish to you on your special day. Your dedication and devotion to our organization over the years will always be remembered and we hope that you will have many happy returns. ... P.S. And a 'happy birthday' wish from Joe Katz."[74]

On May 24, 1973 Henry Hardin "Zipp" Newman turned seventy-nine years old.

In another letter from Ken Smith, Director of the National Football Hall of Fame and Museum, Inc. Cooperstown, New York, Smith wrote:

The 1970s

"Dear Zipp: Thanks for the dandy August 5, 12 and 19 'Dusting 'Em Offs' in the [*Birmingham*] *News*. This is great stuff, who's been around on various corners of the field that Hal [Totten]. Starting with broadcasting the first All Star game. And long before that on the Chicago Daily News. In the booth at Wrigley Field many seasons, then into the front office of the minor leagues. Your columns are first class history stuff and of course go on file in the [National Baseball] Hall of Fame Library. ..."[75]

Sam H. Wallace, Jr., of Birmingham, Alabama on September 1, 1973 wrote a handwritten letter to Goodloe Rutland, President of the Birmingham-Jefferson Civic Center Authority and copied Zipp.

"Dear Mr. Rutland: The Plaza of the Civic Center is not a place to begin economizing. Many people will go to the Exhibition Hall, and some to the Music Hall, and the Theatre; while a throng will gather at the Coliseum, but all will meet and pass through The Plaza. ..."[76]

On the same day Wallace wrote a handwritten letter to Zipp accompanying his letter to Rutland. It read in part:

"Dear Zipp: ... Also, suggested to the Governor, that he make an appropriation for help in building the Coliseum. Maybe a request from you would make more effect. ... Trusting things are going well with you, and your Family, and thanking you again. I remain, Sincerely, Sam H. Wallace, Jr.[77]

E.E. "Rip" Miller, Assistant Director of Athletics, Naval Academy Athletic Association, wrote to Zipp in November.

"Dear Zipp: It was certainly great to hear from you again. I certainly appreciate your story concerning the Alabama/Notre Game battle. Your story brought back many fine memories of my years in football. You did an awful lot of research on the story and you are to be congratulated, but you always were good on detail and, incidentally, <u>correct</u> detail. ... Of course, the highlight to all of us [when visiting Birmingham] was to have had the opportunity to visit Crippled Children's Hospital. ... I sincerely hope that you are enjoying good health and thank you again for sending me your story *Dusting Em Off*."[78]

NFL Referee Tommy Bell

Tommy Bell was a highly respected referee in the National Football League for many years. He came to the NFL from the Southeastern Conference (SEC). Bell always served as a referee. Those old enough will recall Bell's first-down signalling routine. He made a fist with one hand, then slapped that fist into the palm of the other hand, followed by the first-down signal. *Signal, slap, signal.*

On December 3, 1973 Bell, a lawyer at Fowler, Rouse, Measle & Bell, Lexington, Kentucky and not yet retired as a referee of the NFL, wrote:

"Dear Mr. Newman: I received your letter of November 28 with the enclosed correspondence from Reverend William G. West. I enjoyed the quote which you sent for possible use of this and I appreciate you taking the time to send this to me. May I take this opportunity to wish you and yours a most happy holiday season. Very truly yours, Tommy."

The handwritten note at the bottom of the letter read, "My best to your two fine grandsons!!"[79]

1974 Letters

Richard Thigpen, Executive Assistant to the President of the University of Alabama, appears to have written to Zipp within days of meeting up with him, whether at the University, the Goose Dinner, or an A-Day game. This letter's greeting addresses Newman in the Southern style.

"Dear 'Mr.' Zipp:

It was an honor to have you with us for the A-Day football game, and both Dr. Mathews and I were pleased to be able to visit briefly with you outside the elevator prior to kick-off. There is no one in the sports world who has brought more distinction to our state and the University, through the years, than yourself, and all of us in leadership roles here remain deeply mindful of this ...

It is always an honor to have you at the Capstone."[80]

The 1970s

The admiration and attentiveness between Newman and Thigpen was reciprocal. Newman worked with all people in fairness and respect.

Zipp replied to Thigpen's letter of April 30. He wrote on May 14:

> "Dear Doctor 'Richard':
>
> I deeply appreciate your most generous letter.
> Alabama has always been big league in my book and your letter did nothing to mar that image. In fact your letter is the highest compliment I have ever received.
>
> Please accept my congratulations on your richly deserved appointment as Executive Vice President of the University." [81]

There was some level of gamesmanship with the monikers "Mr. Zipp" and "Doctor Richard." It indicates a close enough professional and personal relationship to use it.

Thigpen acknowledged Zipp's congratulations with:

> "Dear Mr. Newman [handwrote Zipp on top of Mr. Newman]:
>
> Thank you for your kind and generous words of congratulations. I appreciate these, more than I can say. I am looking forward to the Goose Dinner, and do hope to see you there."[82]

That same kind of respect and appreciation from Thigpen is evident in a letter from business owner Roy B. Sewell.

> "Dear Zipp:
>
> Thank you for your nice letter and for the pamphlet enclosed. You are a wonderful Christian and a dear friend and I can't tell you how much I appreciate you. I do expect to be in Auburn on May 18 A-Day and I am going to be looking for you.
>
> Hoping everything is fine with you and the family."[83]

Auburn University's A-Day football game was played on May 18, 1974.

Clifford H. Kern, Jr., President, New Orleans Mid-Winter Sports Association, air mailed a letter to Zipp.

> "Dear Zipp: BIRTHDAY GREETINGS! Many happy returns is the sincere wish of every Sugar Bowler, Joe Katz, and Edna Engert. We continuously recall your keen interest in the Sugar Bowl throughout the years and will be forever grateful for the wonderful support you have given us. Have a nice summer and let us hear from you soon."[84]

Zipp turned eighty years old on May 24, 1974.

On Sunday July 21, 1974 *The Birmingham News* printed an article headlined *"Zipp Newman to be cited for service: News sports editor emeritus."* The story made the rounds. That newspaper clipping was included in a letter that Jeff Coleman wrote.[85]

> "Dear Zipp:
>
> Congratulations on your up-coming Day in Knoxville on September 7, 1974. This is wonderful.
>
> You probably knew I was really surprised on the occasion of the [Cecil] Word's wild game dinner. Paul said that he did not know I was to be honored. I appreciate this greatly, particularly, because of you and the Words and those assembled.
>
> Am just back from five days in Boston. Let's be making some plans to go fishing – even if hot summer is not supposed to be the best time.
>
> Your devoted friend, Jeff."[86]

The day after the article appeared in *The News*, James E. Vance, Senior Vice President of The First National Bank of Birmingham wrote:

> "Dear Zipp:
>
> Congratulations on the fine honor you will receive on September 7 in Knoxville. This is certainly well-deserved and your many friends are delighted to see you so recognized.

With best personal regards, I am Sincerely, Jim."[87]

On September 7, 1974 the University of Tennessee honored Henry Hardin "Zipp" Newman in Knoxville. *The News* article of July 21 read in part:

> "The September 7 Saturday when Tennessee and UCLA launch the 1974 NCAA College Football TV series will be "Zipp Newman Day" in Knoxville, the site of the game.

> "The East Tennessee chapter of the National Football Hall of Fame Foundation will host a luncheon, four hours before the late afternoon kickoff for national cameras, with the 80-year old Birmingham News sports editor emeritus honored guest.

> "[Bob Woodruff, Athletic Director of the University of Tennessee and event organizer said] We have a tremendous crowd to pay tribute to Zipp. For what he has done for college athletics he deserves every nice thing we could give him."

The Long Over-Due Tribute
Ralph "Shug" Jordan, head football coach, Auburn University, wrote to Zipp on October 25, 1974.

> "Dear Zipp:

> I have just learned that you have been selected along with six other outstanding sportsmen to the Alabama Sports Hall of Fame. Nothing could give me greater pleasure than to write and offer my sincere congratulations to you on this high honor.

> "I cannot think of anyone who is more richly deserving of this recognition. In my opinion, it is a long over-due tribute to you for all that you have done in behalf of sports over the years. ..."[88]

Another Nomination Letter
H.B. "Mac" McElroy at Texas A&M University in College Station, Texas wrote:

> "Dear Zipp:

My nephew, Truman Jones, Jr., who is with Vulcan Materials Co. in Birmingham, sent me your column of September 8, relating to Homer Norton.

It gave me great pleasure to know that there is at least one other man who holds the late Homer Hill Norton in such high esteem …

Now you get him into the Alabama Sports Hall of Fame and we will have covered them [other halls of fame] all."

McElroy and Wilbur Evans wrote the book *The Twelfth Man*.[89]

1975 Letters

On February 3, 1975 Wilbur H. Hutsell, Track Coach Emeritus, Auburn University, wrote:

"Dear Henry:

I'm so happy that you are being inducted into the Alabama Sports Hall of Fame. It was not Governor Wallace who was the father of the organization – it is your baby.

I shall always be indebted to you for my 56 years of happiness in Alabama. You helped me weather storms in the early days at Auburn. The BAC days were happy ones, but at times, hard. There has never been a time in 56 years that I could not lean on you. Your guiding influence provided me with the <u>Coach of the Years</u> trophy. Induction into the Helms Hall of Fame and the ASHF [ASHOF] were your products, too.

Walking in a rough area, at night, or where there are steps in the Parliament House and the Civic Center is quite an ordeal for me, so I'm passing up the invitation on the 13 and 14. During the ceremonies I will be praying for your health and happiness.

Sincerely, Wilbur" [90]

1977 Letters

Dwight Keith wrote on *Coach & Athlete* stationery, a general letter on February 23, 1977 addressed to REGION COLUMNISTS AND MEMBERS OF ADVISORY BOARD announcing that,

"As of February 7, 1977, I am no longer associated with COACH & ATHLETE Magazine. Henceforth, I do not wish to take credit or blame for the actions or policies of the new publisher."

He included a three-page handwritten note to Zipp.

"Dear Zipp – after 39 years with *Coach & Athlete* I took my leave. Enjoyed it most of the way. I hope you are feeling well. Your many favors are remembered, and your friendship is cherished. ... Thanks for your friendship and may God bless you. Cordially, Dwight."[91]

Henry Hardin "Zipp" Newman, on Thursday March 3, 1977, passed away. According to his son-in-law, Walter Morris [Sr.], Zipp expected to be out of the hospital within a few days. But such was not the case. Zipp was survived by his wife, Frances Newman and their two daughters, Mrs. Meredith Newman Looney of Sewanee, Tennessee and Mrs. Frances Newman Morris of Mountain Brook, Alabama.

Many civic organizations honored Zipp Newman over the years, not only for his sports reporting but for his humanitarian projects. We do not think that Zipp would select any one of his humanitarian projects as his favorite. In sports, yes, he preferred baseball over football – he was the official scorer for the Southern League's Birmingham games for forty-four years.

He is fondly and gratefully remembered for the Crippled Children's Clinic and Hospital, the Alabama Sight Conservation Association, his fight against tuberculosis, and his dream of creating a sports hall of fame for the State of Alabama.

The last case of polio [and smallpox] recorded in the United States of America was in 1979.[92] Henry Hardin "Zipp" Newman would have rejoiced.

---

[1] George Gardner, Secretary, Football Officials Association, Southeastern Conference. Typed on organization letterhead. January 9, 1970.
[2] National Football Foundation bio of George Gardner. https://footballfoundation.org/roster.aspx?rp_id=310
[3] Don E. Liebendorfer. Historian, Department of Physical Education and Athletics, Stanford University. Typed on university letterhead. January 27, 1970.
[4] Don E. Liebendorfer. Historian, Department of Physical Education and Athletics, Stanford University. Typed on university letterhead. January 27, 1970.
[5] Don E. Liebendorfer. Stanford University. Typed on university letterhead. March 2, 1970.

6 Don E. Liebendorfer. Historian, Department of Physical Education and Athletics, Stanford University. Typed on university letterhead. March 4, 1970.
7 Don E. Liebendorfer. *The Color of Life Is Red: A History of Stanford University Athletics 1892-1971*. Palo Alto, California: Stanford University Department of Athletics, 1972), ix.
8 Tom Willingham, Typed letter on plain paper. no address. February 25, 1970.
9 Alabama High School Football Historical Society. http://www.ahsfhs.org/coaches/coachestop.asp?Coach=H.L.%20Shorty%20Ogle
10 Tennessee Sports Hall of Fame. Raymond Johnson. http://tshf.net/halloffame/johnson-raymond/
11 Raymond Johnson. No address, but Tennessee. Typed on his "fancy" plain paper. February 26, 1970.
12 Raymond Johnson, Sports Editor, *The Nashville Tennessean*. Typed on company letterhead. May 9, 1970.
13 Raymond Johnson, Sports Editor, *The Nashville Tennesseean*. Typed on company letterhead. May 23, 1970.
14 Raymond Johnson. Director of Publicity. Churchill Downs. Typed on organization letterhead. August 24, 1972.
15 Raymond Johnson. Churchill Downs. Typed on stationery of Quality Inn/West, Memphis, Tennessee. September [no day], 1972.
16 W.R. "Bill" Schroeder, Managing Director, Helms Athletic Foundation – Helms Hall. Typed on organization letterhead. March 2, 1970.
17 W.R. "Bill" Schroeder, Managing Director, Helms Foundation. Typed on organization letterhead. June 16, 1970.
18 W.R. "Bill" Schroeder, Managing Director, Helms Foundation. Typed on organization letterhead. June 17, 1970
19 Braven Dyer. Typed on plain paper. May 4, 1970.
20 W.R. "Bill" Schroeder, Managing Director, Helms Foundation. Typed on organization letterhead. June 30, 1970
21 Dwight Keith. "Joe Guyon." *Coach and Athlete* magazine. April 30, 1970.
22 Joe Guyon. https://en.wikipedia.org/wiki/Joe_Guyon
23 William Heymans, Secretary-Treasurer, Chicago Cubs, Inc. Typed on company letterhead. May 15, 1970.
24 W.H. Hutsell, Auburn University. Typed on Athletic Department letterhead. June 3, 1970.
25 V.L. "Spud" Davis. Typed on plain paper. July 22, 1970.
26 Ed McKeever, Chief Talent Scout, The Boston Patriots Football Club. Typed on club letterhead. October 28, 1970.
27 Michael C. Matsos, Birmingham, Alabama. Typed on Michael's Enterprises letterhead. September 28, 1970.
28 Ed Leigh McMillan. Chairman of the Board, T.R. Miller Mill Company, Inc., Brewton, Alabama. Typed on company letterhead. November 3, 1970.
29 http://www.ahsfhs.org/bowls/CrippledChildren.asp
30 Water R. Bogart, Jr. Alexandria, Virginia. Typed on personal letterhead as Colonel Walter R. Bogart, Jr. January 9, 1971.
31 C.H. Pearson. Pearson Advertising Agency, Inc., NYC. Typed on agency letterhead. January 27, 1970.
32 Lloyd Gregory. Lloyd Gregory & Associates, Houston, TX. Typed on company letterhead, February 9, 1971.
33 Frank Wallace, University of Notre Dame Library. Typed on university letterhead. April 30, 1971.
34 Roger Kiley. Judge, 7th Circuit, United States Court of Appeals, Chicago. Typed on Court letterhead. June 6, 1971.
35 Notre Dame Football Review 1919. http://archives.nd.edu/Football/Football-1919.pdf.
36 Tram Sessions. Liberty National Life Insurance Company, Birmingham. Typed on company letterhead. June 16, 1971.

The 1970s

37 Tram Sessions. https://en.wikipedia.org/wiki/Tram_Sessions

38 Roy B. Sewell. Chairman, Sewell Manufacturing Company, Bremen, Georgia. Typed on company letterhead. July 6, 1971.

39 W.H. Hutsell. Athletic Department, Auburn University. Typed on university letterhead. September 9, 1971.

40 Jack Meagher. https://en.wikipedia.org/wiki/Jack_Meagher

41 Robert Jemison, Jr. President, Jemison Realty Company, Inc. Typed on company letterhead. November 16, 1971.

42 Dwight Keith. Born in Argo, Alabama 1900. Sells *Coach and Athlete* magazine in 1972. Source is long letter written to his daughter, Carolita (Carole Lita). Typed on plain paper.

43 Gabriel Paul. President, Cleveland Indians, Inc. Typed on company letterhead. January 4, 1972.

44 Nell Coleman Ennis. Livingston, Alabama. Handwritten note which included a cut-out article on Jeff Colemen dated February 20, 1972.

45 Jefferson J. Coleman. Secretary, The University of Alabama National Alumni Association. Typed on association letterhead. March 22, 1972.

46 Jefferson Coleman. An Invitation to the Zipp Newman Fishing Festival. April 24, 1972.

47 Jefferson J. Coleman. Secretary, The University of Alabama National Alumni Association. Typed on association letterhead. May 30, 1972.

48 Eloise Metzger Cooper. Forest Park, Georgia. Typed on plain paper. March 30, 1972.

49 A.M. "Tony" Ulrich. Custodian and Director, Dick Lamb Football Collection. Typed on Football Information Bureau letterhead. April 15, 1972.

50 A.M. "Tony" Ulrich. Custodian and Director of the Dick lamb Football Collection, Dayton, Ohio. Handwritten on bureau letterhead. April 25, 1972.

51 A.M. "Tony" Ulrich. Custodian and Director of the Dick lamb Football Collection, Dayton, Ohio. Handwritten on bureau letterhead. May 14, 1972.

52 A.M. "Tony" Ulrich. Custodian and Director of the Dick Lamb Collection at the Football Information Bureau. Handwritten on organization letterhead. August 26, 1972.

53 A.M. "Tony" Ulrich. Football Information Bureau, Dayton, Ohio. Typed on organization letterhead. October 10, 1972.

54 A.M. "Tony" Ulrich. Football Information Bureau, Dayton. Ohio. Handwritten on organization letterhead. December 24, 1972.

55 Floyd H. Mann. Special Assistant to the President, The University of Alabama. Typed on university letterhead. June 9, 1972.

56 Richard Thigpen letter to Zipp Newman. The University of Alabama. June 13, 1972.

57 Tonto Coleman. Commissioner, The Southeastern Conference, Birmingham, Alabama. Typed on conference letterhead. July 5, 1972.

58 C.H. Pearson. Pearson Advertising Agency Inc. Typed on agency letterhead. July 11, 1972.

59 https://www.baseball-reference.com/register/player.fcgi?id=kakoli001the

60 Frank A. Wagner. Director of the Birmingham Park & Recreation Board. Typed on board letterhead. July 27, 1972.

61 George R. Woodruff. Director,Department of Athletics, The University of Tennessee. Typed on department letterhead. July 31, 1972. [See https://www.youtube.com/watch?v=xcoCFpPjGpM]

62 Archie R. Dykes. Chancellor. The University of Tennessee. Typed on university letterhead. September 19, 1972

63 Robert, B. Scheffing. Vice President and General Managers – New York National League Baseball Club [The Mets]. Typed on club letterhead. August 8, 1972.

64 Elbert S. Jemison, Jr. President & Treasurer. Jemison Securities Corporation, Birmingham. Typed on company letterhead. August 22, 1972.

65 Paul M. Grist. Selma, Alabama. Typed on personal letterhead. September 28, 1972.

66 Ken Smith. Director. National Baseball Hall of Fame and Museum, Inc. Cooperstown, NY. Typed on organization letterhead. November 1, 1972.

The 1970s

67 Bob Shepherd. Shepherd Realty Company, Inc. Birmingham, Alabama. Handwritten on company letterhead. November 28, 1972.

68 Sammy Barnes, Louisville, Mississippi. Excellently hand-written on plain paper. February 7, 1973.

69 Hoyt Winslett, Jr. Episcopal Church of the Nativity, Huntsville, Alabama. Typed on church letterhead.February 16, 1973.

70 Hoyt Winslett [Sr.]. President. Dollarhide Camp, Inc. "Hunting and Fishing Preserve in Greene County, Alabama." Handwritten on camp letterhead. February 27, 1973.

71 W.H. "Wilbur" Hutsell. Auburn University. Typed on university letterhead. February 21, 1973.

72 Richard Thigpen. Executive Assistant to the President of the University of Alabama. Typed, cc on plain paper. February 28, 1973.

73 J. Luther "Luke" Sewell, Akron, Ohio. Typed on personal letterhead. March 2, 1973.

74 John W. Boebinger, President – New Orleans Mid-Winter Sports Association. Typed on association letterhead. May 22, 1973.

75 Ken Smith. Director, National Baseball Hall of Fame and Museum, Inc., Cooperstown, New York. Typed on organization letterhead. August 25, 1973.

76 Sam H. Wallace, Jr., Birmingham, Alabama. Separate handwritten letters to Goodoe Rutland, Civic Center, and copied Zipp Newman. Written on plain paper. September 1, 1973.

77 Sam H. Wallace, Jr., Birmingham, Alabama. Separate handwritten letter to Zipp Newman. Written on plain paper. September 1, 1973.

78 E.E. "Rip" Miller, Assistant Director of Athletics, U.S Naval Academy, Typed on athletic association letterhead. November 27, 1973.

79 Thomas B. "Tommy" Bell, former NFL referee and attorney at Fowler, Rouse, Measle & Bell. Typed on firm's letterhead with a short, handwritten note at bottom. December 3, 1973.

80 Richard Thigpen. Executive Assistant to the President of The University of Alabama. Typed on university letterhead. April 30, 1974.

81 Henry Hardin "Zipp" Newman letter to Richard Thigpen. Typed on *The Birmingham News* letterhead. May 16, 1974.

82 Richard Thigpen. Executive Vice President, The University of Alabama. Typed on university letterhead. May 23, 1974.

83 Roy B. Sewell. Chairman, Sewell Manufacturing Company, Bremen, Georgia. Typed on company letterhead. April 30, 1974.

84 Clifford H. Kern, Jr. President – New Orleans Mid-Winter Sports Association. Typed on organization letterhead May 22, 1974.

85 *The Birmingham News*. Article "News sports editor emeritus – Zipp Newman to be cited for service" in Tennessee. Page 4-C. July 211, 1974.

86 Jeff Coleman, Consultant. Typed on Jefferson J. Coleman letterhead, University, Alabama 35486. July 21, 1974.

87 James E. Vance. Senior Vice President – The First National Bank of Birmingham. Typed on bank letterhead. July 22, 1974.

88 Ralph "Shug" Jordan. Head Football Coach, Auburn University. Typed on university letterhead. October 25, 1974.

89 H. B. McElroy. College Station, Texas. Typed on personal letterhead. November 27, 1974.

90 Wilbur H. Hutsell, Track Coach Emeritus, Auburn University. Typed on university letterhead. February 3, 1975.

91 Dwight Keith. Founder of Coach & Athlete Magazine. Formal note typed on magazine letterhead. handwritten note to Zipp on bottom and back on announcement. February 23, 1977.

92 Last cases of polio recorded in the United States of America. https://www.cdc.gov/polio/us

Zipp's Self-Assessment Letter

One of the few letters archived and written by Newman is addressed to Mr. Giles Baker of Birmingham, Alabama. The typed letter is dated March 19, 1948 on stationery of *The Birmingham News/The Birmingham Age-Herald*. Perhaps Newman is responding to a request, or perhaps the addressee is fictitious, allowing Zipp to document his achievements.

March 19, 1948
Mr. Giles Baker,
Birmingham, Ala.

Dear Giles,

Here's the information on yours truly.
35-years of experiencing writing sports for The Birmingham News.
Named sports editor in 1919 – dean of Southern writers.

Has seen more New Year's Day bowl games as a visiting writer than any other man in football. Rose, Sugar, Cotton, Orange and the first and last New Year's Day game[1] in Havanna [sic], Cuba.

Holds record for having scored more consecutive years as an official scorer in baseball than any other scorer. 29 years. Helped to write the scoring guide for Minor League clubs – 48.

Has written sports stories for Esquire, Sport, Baseball Digest, Sporting News and College Humor. Served as an advisor to Christy Walsh and Grantland Rice on southern sports. Ghosted Frank Thomas' All-American [sic] series.

Member of Collier's All-America Football Board.
First president of Southern Football and Baseball Writers' Associations, first president of Federation of Baseball Writers. Member of Football Writers Association.

---

[1] On December 7, 1946 in Havana, Cuba, Mississippi Southern College defeated the University of Havana 55-0 in the Bacardi Bowl (also referred to as the Rhumba Bowl and Cigar Bowl). This is probably the game mentioned in the letter.

Possesses the outstanding sports library in the field of sports writing. Office is a Sport Gallery, pronounced by visiting sports writers as the only one of its kind in America. Brown-Bigelow are [sic] literally represented in the library and [sic] the color section.

For three years was most often quoted Sports Writer in the Country in Eddie Brietz's Associated Press column. Organized Birmingham's Monday Morning Quarterback club – famed for helping raise money for the Crippled Children's Clinic – and bringing famous men in football to Birmingham.

Has served in an unofficial capacity as an advisor to the Sugar Bowl, the Orange Bowl and the Dixie Bowl. Has been appearing on National Broadcasts as guest of Bill Stern, Red Barber and Harry Wismer and Mel Allen on bowl games and World's [sic] Series games.

A close friend of Commissioner Happy Chandler, George Troutman and Ford [sic] Frisch.[1]

Originated and got the Birmingham News to sponsor Crippled Children's Clinic football game for a new hospital – more than a million and half already raised.

East-West boys baseball double-header for Better Hearing Clinic in Medical Center in Birmingham.

All-College basketball double-header for Better Hearing Clinic in Medical Center.

Negro High School football game for TB Clinic.

One of the writers' [sic] hobbies has been collecting data on famous places in sports. Has been running a series in paper.

He can give as referenced:
Grantland Rice, New York, New York

---

[1] Frank Frisch, more likely. Frisch played baseball for the New York Giants and St. Louis Cardinals. He managed the St. Louis Cardinals, Pittsburgh Pirates, and the Chicago Cubs.

Christy Walsh, Hollywood, Calif.
Bill Stern, Director of Sports for NBC, New York.
Red Barber, Director of Sports for CBS, New York.
Harry Wismer, Director of Sports for ABC, New York.
Mel Allen, Movietone narrator and announcer for New York Yankees'
[sic] baseball and football games, Yankee Stadium, New York.
Chest Smith, Sports Editor, Pittsburgh Press, Pittsburgh, Pa.
Arch Ward, Sports Editor, Chicago Tribune, Chicago, Ill.
Paul Zimmerman, Sports Editor, Los Angeles Times, Los Angeles.
Braven Dyer, feature sports writer, Los Angeles Times, Los Angeles.
Harry G. Salinger, Sports Editor, Detroit News, Detroit, Mich.
Frank Menke, New York City.
Frank Leahy, Coach of Notre Dame.
Herman Hickman, Coach of Yale.
Wallace Wade, Coach of Duke.
Lynn Waldorf, Coach of California.
Billy Southworth, manager of Boston Braves.
Sec Taylor, Des Moines Register, Des Moines, Iowa.
George Barton, Star Journal & Tribune, Minneapolis, Min.
Robert Hooey, Ohio State Journal, Columbus, Ohio
Bill Cunningham, Boston Herald, Boston, Mass.
Ted Smits, Sports Editor, Associated Press, New York City.
Clyde McBride, Kansas City Star, Kansas City, Kan.
Sam Leavy, Journal, Milwaukee.

Goes to Minor League meetings, All-Star football game in Chicago.
Knows outstanding sports writers in every section of country –
meeting 'em at the biggest sporting events.

I hope I haven't bored you too much ---
Zipp Newman[1]

---

[1] Zipp Newman letter addressed to Giles Baker, Birmingham, Ala., dated March 19, 1948 and typed on stationery of *The Birmingham News/The Birmingham Age-Herald*. Five pages original, transcribed here. This could have been a "practice" letter of self-assessment. There are many misspelled words.

Honors, Awards and Recognitions

1945   Silver Service Medal – Birmingham Kiwanis Club

1945   Newsweek Magazine published special article on Newman's activities on behalf of underprivileged children and Alabama's health

1948   Honorary Membership – American Hospital Association

1948   Honored for Service to underprivileged children of Alabama by the Downtown Lion's Club

1968   Honorary Membership in newly-formed Birmingham Press Club

1968   Executive Secretary Alabama Sports Hall of Fame

1974   Zipp Newman Day in Knoxville, Tennessee

1975   Induction into Alabama Sports Hall of Fame

1976   President of Southern Football Sports Writers Association; Southern Baseball Sports Writers Association; National Minor League Baseball Sports Writers Association

Longest-serving official scorer of Southern [Baseball] Association for Birmingham games

41 years of serving on selection committees for National Football Hall of Fame; Jockey Hall of Fame; Golf Hall of Fame's Athlete of the Year

Served with Grantland Rice on All-America Football Board

1979   Stained glass windows in honor of Henry Hardin "Zipp" Newman were placed in the hospital chapel at The University of Alabama at Birmingham. A handwritten note from UAB's Chancellor to Mrs. Newman included pictures of the windows.

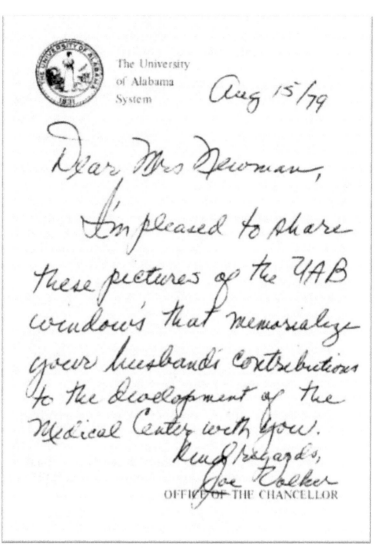

The University
of Alabama
System

Aug 15/79

Dear Mrs Newman,

I'm pleased to share these pictures of the UAB windows that memorialize your husbands contributions to the development of the Medical Center with you.

Kind Regards,

Joe Volker

OFFICE OF THE CHANCELLOR

These stained glass windows
originally hung in the

Zipp Newman Chapel

of the

Crippled Children's Clinic and Hospital

(1951 – 1969)

named in honor of the late

Henry Hardin "Zipp" Newman

(1894 – 1977)

Sports Editor of The Birmingham News

from 1919 – 1959

Wording on a plaque in the President's Conference Room
Mortimer Jordan Hall, The University of Alabama in Birmingham
Presented to Mrs. Zipp Newman on June 26, at Birmingham, Alabama, 1979

Joseph F. Volker, Chancellor
The University of Alabama System

S. Richardson Hill, Jr., M.D., President

143

Summary of Letters

Cox, Ted	**1935-02-18** Head Football Coach at Tulane University responds to Zipp about his scoring system package
Davis, Allen	**1968-11-13** Davis Brothers Farm Danville, KY. About a *Sports Illustrated* article about Bo McMillan.
Davis, Virgil Lawrence "Spud"	**1970-07-22** Writes Zipp about previous Sunday's article on Alabama's All-Time Major League Club. Davis, a Birmingham native played for Cardinals, Phillies, Reds, and Pirates.
Drew, H.D.	**1935-02-02** University of Alabama Athletic Association, replies to Zipp about his scoring chart.
	1971-05-04 Writes handwritten letter to Zipp – enjoyed seeing Zipp but turns down invitation to fishing trip.
Dyer, Braven	**1970-05-04** West Coast journalist writes that he saw Dixie Howell at our annual HoF dinner. Looking forward to UA-USC meeting in September.
Dykes, Archie R.	**1972-09-19** Chancellor, University of Tennessee Regrets that Zipp unable to attend event
Engert, Edna	**1968-10-11** Sugar Bowl committee; enclosed $5.95 for Zipp's new book
Ennis, Nell Coleman	**1972-02-20** Writes about Jeff Coleman with article
Farley, Joe	**1968-05-01** President Alabama Power Co., Thanks Zipp for series of articles in *The Birmingham News* on reservoirs in Alabama
Farr, Herbert "Bones"	**1969-02-13** Recent Alabama Sports Hall of Fame Induction was wonderful and organized. Shocked by utter disregard for John E. "Boozer" Pitts
Ford Motor Company	**1935-03-04** Writer says Dizzy Dean wrote Mr. Ford on behalf of Zipp regarding a sports feature to be added to our broadcasting feature of the World Series – signature illegible
Gardner, George	**1970-01-09** Secretary SEC Football Officials Association – We will miss you at our annual party
Gregory, Lloyd	**1971-02-09** Lloyd Gregory & Associates., Houston, TX – about 1928 Dixie Series between Birmingham Barons and Houston Buffaloes – Ray Caldwell and Dizzy Dean
Gregory, Wallace	**1971-04-30** Alabama Sports Hall of Fame; Hank Crisp; Dixie Howell
Grist, Paul M.	**1972-09-28** – Past District Governor – ROTARY INT'L. Writes a letter of promotion for William Gray Little for Alabama Sports Hall of Fame
Harper, Cliff	**1954-11-04** Executive Secretary AHSAA – Thanks Zipp for talk given at Montgomery [AL] Quarterback Club
Herndon, John	**1969-08-21** addressed to Bill Streit about Zipp's book *Impact of Southern Football*

LETTER WRITER	CONTEXT
Heyman, William	**1970-05-15** Chicago National League Baseball Club, Secy-Treas – acknowledges receipt of Zipp's article sent to Mr. Wrigley
Hickey, Bill	**1954-06-03** WCBS-TV Thanks Zipp for all he did for Hickey
Hill, Henry William	**1968-09-15** Mooresville, AL; corrects Zipp on an article on Sunday the 15th
Holt, Thad	**1973-04-17** Letter to Ford Frick, cc: Zipp; enclosed Newman column; See Red Barber story.
Hudgins, Elmore	**1969-07-15** Public Information Officer SEC – "committee of seven" all-time football team – offer to submit names
Hutsell, W.H.	**1969-01-28** About Tallulah Bankhead's death **1969-02-27** Replies to Zipp's letter. Homer Swingle. Goose Dinner looking forward **1969-06-16** On Sunday article – boat sinking **1969-09-17** Grateful for our 50 years of friendship **1970-06-03** Athletic Department, Auburn University – Sorry you couldn't be here for A-Day; article about Howard Hill **1971-09-06** Train ride – John Bradberry article in Opelika-Auburn Sunday newspaper **1973-02-21** About Hutsell's wife Corinne's death – and Zipp-Wilbur 54-year friendship **1975-02-03** Happy about inductions into Alabama Sports Hall of Fame. "It was not Governor Wallace who was the father ... - it is your baby."
Innis, Frances	**1954-05-16** Thank you note with a Braven Dyer article in *Los Angeles Times*
James, Fob, Jr.	**1968-03-11** "I deeply appreciate your kind words ..." *Birmingham News* article
Jemison, Elbert S., Jr.	**1972-08-22** President & Treasurer Jemison Securities, Birmingham, Alabama
Jemison, Robert, Jr	**1971-11-16** about death of Bishop Clingman in Louisville
Johnson, Raymond	**1970-02-26** apologizes for his Alabama Sports Hall of Fame absence due to illness; Tennessee Sports Hall of Fame (TnSHOF) dinner on Feb 20 went well **1970-05-09** About his becoming Executive Secretary of Tennessee Sports Hall of Fame **1970-05-23** Sports Editor at *The Nashville Tennessean* – Does not want Executive Secretary job of new TnSHOF **1972-08-24** Director of Publicity at Churchill Downs **1972-09-01** On Quality Inn/West stationery, Memphis – writes Zipp to say he is representing Baseball Writers Association at the American Legion World Series

LETTER WRITER	CONTEXT
Jordan, Ralph	**1968-07-23** AU football coach – Thanks for letter; feeling much better.
	1974-10-25 Congrats on selection to Alabama Sports Hall of Fame
Keeler, O.B.	**1934-11-21** *The Atlanta Journal* responding to Zipp's scoring system package
Keith, Dwight	**1959-01-01** Zipp to Dwight Keith - NO DATE – Zipp typed "Wednesday"
	1963-05-21 Article written by Zipp about Keith
	1970-04-30 Asked Zipp for football stats on Joe Guyon
	1977-02-23 Addressed "TO REGION COLUMNISTS AND MEMBERS OF THE ADVISORY BOARD" of Coach & Athlete Magazine. As of 2-7-1977 no longer associated with C&A. Attached a long, handwritten letter to Zipp
Kern, Clifford H., Jr.	**1974-05-22** Birthday greetings to Zipp from Sugar Bowl people
Kiley, Roger Joseph	**1971-06-01** Federal Judge in Chicago; Notre Dame football player referenced "Tommy" from Porter Grant, *Birmingham News* sports sheet
Klein, Larry	**1969-09-05** Director of National Collegiate Sports Services – Thanks for All-America Football Team story – will place into Sports Kit to other writers
Liebendorfer, Don E.	**1970-01-27** Good friend USMC Major Dennis A. Cavagnaro – your column of January 18 – wants a copy
	1970-01-27 addressed to Cavagnaro – re: Stanford never beating University of Alabama
	1970-03-02 Thanks for sending presentation given at Alabama Sports Hall of Fame. Thanks for never forgetting me
	1970-03-04 Thanks for tear sheets of tributes to Hank Crisp. Your continued thoughtfulness is appreciated
Little, Louis	**1935-02-19** Department of Physical Education, Columbia U, NYC – about Zipp's scoring system
	1935-03-04 "I would be more than happy to help you ..."
Madigan, E.P.	**1935-02-12** Director of Physical Education Saint Mary's College, CA – about Zipp's scoring system
Mann, Floyd H.	**1972-06-09** Special Assistant to President University of Alabama; Scottsboro meeting about your great contributions
Martin, Donald	**1969-11-14** Department of English Auburn University – Moose Clabaugh asked to contact you
Martin, John D.	**1920-04-12** President – Southern Assoc of BB Clubs: Congrats succeeding Henry Vance
	1924-01-10 President – Southern Association – thanks for Jan 7 letter

	1924-04-12 Pres – SABBC – Reappointment for 1924 baseball season scorer in Birmingham
Matson, Michael C.	**1970-09-28** Michael's Enterprises Birmingham to Thomas J Hamilton, PAC-8 Conference, cc: Zipp – thanks for Rose Bowl Stadium picture and list of SEC teams who have played in the Rose Bowl Game
McDowell, Jimmie	**1969-02-11** to Earle Edwards from Jimmie McDowell. National Football HoF. Mentions Zipp, Dwight Keith, Reed Green, etc.
McElroy, H.B.	**1974-11-27** Nephew sent Zipp article on Homer Norton dated September 8. Wrote about his book with Wilbur Evans, too.
McGrane, Bert	**1969-08-03** Football Writers Association Secretary-Treasurer: get out of your rocking chair – name the all-time team
McGugin, Dan	**1927-06-11** Atty – McGugin, Evans & Cate, former Vandy coach – congratulations on marriage
	1934-11-15 Director of Athletics Vanderbilt Univ. Football talk
	1934-11-15 Second letter of the day regarding Zipp's scoring system
McKeever, Ed	**1970-10-28** Boston Patriots chief talent scout; daughter sent article. Thanks for your article about me.
McMillan, Ed Leigh	**1970-11-03** Chairman, T.R. Miller Mill Company, Inc., Brewton, AL. Donation to Crippled Children's Clinic Football Game.
Meagher, Jack	**1935-03-06** Football Coach API or Auburn – about Zipp's scoring system
Mehre, Harry	**1935-02-07** Dept Athletics UGA – about Zipp's scoring system
Miller, E.E. "Rip"	**1973-11-27** Asst Dir of Athletics USNA – refers to article sent by Zipp about Notre Dame/Alabama battle
Montgomery, R. Ames	**1924-11-16** Pres - Centre College; thanks for article about his football team after beating University of Alabama
NBC	**1935-02-12** Comments about Zipp's scoring system; probably from Don Thompson
Neely, Jess	**1969-11-12** Dept Athletics Vanderbilt University – Thanks for copy of Zipp's book
Neyland, R.R.	**1948-05-24** Copy of letter sent to Walter Stewart – cc Zipp in 1951
	1951-03-05 Director of Athletics at University of Tennessee – comments about the two-platoon system
Nichols, Bill	**1968-07-12** US Congress 4th District Alabama – re: Don Drennen and Dr. Walter B. Jones, State Geologist

LETTER WRITER	CONTEXT
Nixon, Richard M.	**1969-10-23** Followed Zipp's columns for year – "Impact of Southern Football"
O'Brien, Mickey	**1969-09-26** Trainer University of Tennessee – thanks for article of August 24 about me and other trainers
Parker, John M.G.	**1951-12-05** Congratulations to Zipp on award as "Papa" of Crippled Children's Clinic
Parker, P.B.	**1935-02-07** Director of Athletics at University of Tennessee – comments on Zipp's scoring system
Paterson, Will	**1927-04-07** Rosemont Gardens, Montgomery, Alabama. Thanks for writing about Jim
Paul, Gabriel	**1969-05-16** President – Cleveland Indians, Inc. Will dig up pictures of Joe and Luke Sewell, and Tris Speaker.
	1972-01-04 about Satchel Paige induction to Alabama Sports Hall of Fame on January 14
Pearson, C.H.	**1971-01-27** Pearson Advertising Agency, NYC – Requests permission to reprint Zipp's article on "The Modern Football Team"
	1972-07-11 Pearson Adv. Co, NYC – Thank you for June 25 article; also mentions Ted Kaicoliris
Pelkin, Dwight	**1935-01-03** 15-year-old wants a "southern write-up" of the recent Rose Bowl game from Zipp
Peoples, W.G. "Pete"	**1969-09-19** Southern Pacific Company. Just read "Dusting em off" for Sept. 14. Sorry you cannot come out here to my retirement dinner. You were gracious in your article.
	1970-01-20 Just received book "*Impact of Southern Football*"
Pratt, James B.	**1969-02-14** Congratulations on the first Alabama Sports Hall of Fame; glad to see uncle Derrill Pratt was one of the nominees
Rice, Grantland	**1934-11-09** Editor, *The American Golfer*. Radio broadcasting slants/perspectives.
	1935-02-27 The American Golfer – comments on Zipp's scoring system
	1935-02-27 Rice's plans about radio – hooked up with W.W. Wells on the football guide
Robert, L.W. Junior	**1966-02-28** Reply to a letter from Zipp. Rose Bowl 1929; Bobby Jones
Russell, Torance	**1969-02-11** Alabama Sports Hall of Fame Induction Dinner. Thank you for the part you played
Scheffing, Robert B.	**1972-08-08** NY Mets Vice President & General Manager. Responds to Zipp's request to schedule Casey Stengel.
Schroeder, W.H.	**1970-07-16** Managing Director – Helms Athletic Foundation – hope to make the UA-USC game
	1970-07-17 Refers book – Deke Houlgate "Football Thesaurus"

1970-07-30 Managing Director – Delighted to learn that Alabama Sports Hall of Fame extended an offer to Braven Dyer to attend Alabama-Southern California football game, all expenses paid

1970-03-02 Reply to Zipp's note – plaque to Alabama Sports Hall of Fame

Sehrt, Clem — **1966-06-09** President National American Bank of New Orleans – Asks Zipp for influence with William Elton "Bucky" Moore of McComb, Mississippi nomination for National Football Hall of Fame

Seibels, George W. — **1969-03-19** Mayor of Birmingham to Frank House – Congratulations on legislative work on Alabama Sports Hall of Fame. Cc: Alabama Sports Hall of Fame Board

Sessions, Tram — **1971-06-16** Officer at Liberty National Life Insurance Co., Birmingham and former Secretary Treasurer of Alabama Sports Hall of Fame: "Sorry, no money" to contribute this year

Sewell, Luther "Luke" — **1973-03-02** Thanks for Zipp's help on being inducted to Alabama Sports Hall of Fame

Sewell, Roy — **1968-04-10** President Sewell Manufacturing Company Bremen, GA. Thanks for *Book of Common Prayer*

1968-10-12 Glad you liked the suit. I appreciate your friendship

1969-09-17 Thank you for "Impact of Southern Football"

1971-07-06 Nice writeup in your June 30th column

1974-04-30 Thanks for letter. Looking for you at Auburn A-Day on May 18

Shaughnessy, Clark — **1966-05-16** LA, Calif. About April issue of *Coach & Athlete Magazine* about Dan McGugin

1968-02-24 about December 1967 C&A article on Shaughnessy

Shepherd, Robert W. — **1972-11-28** Shepherd Realty-Birmingham; About recent article about his father by Zipp

Siler, Tom — **1969-05-16** Reporter, *Knoxville Sentinel* – sent article about the 1901 University of Tennessee – University of Alabama game – see Nash Buckingham on same game called for "darkness"

Smith, Ken — **1972-11-01** Director National Baseball Hall of Fame and Museum, Cooperstown, NY: Did you ever get to visit with Phil Cavaretta?

1973-08-25 About articles by Zipp on August 5, 12, and 19

Sparkman, John — **1970-01-26** U.S Senator from Alabama. "Glad to see copy of your letter from President Nixon."

LETTER WRITER	CONTEXT
Stephenson, Stuart	**1935-02-25** *The Montgomery Advertiser* – About Zipp's scoring system
Thigpen, Richard	**1972-06-13** Executive Assistant to President University of Alabama – Goose Dinner, Cecil Word
	1973-02-28 Letter to Cecil Word, copies Zipp
	1974-04-30 Good to have you at A-Day football game
	1974-05-16 From Zipp congratulations to Thigpen for promotion as Executive Vice President at University of Alabama
	1974-05-23 Thank you letter about promotion to Executive Vice President. Looking forward to next Goose Dinner in Scottsboro
Thomas, Frank	**1935-02-07** Football Coach University of Alabama – comments on Zipp's scoring system
Ulrich, A.M. "Tony"	**1972-04-15** Letter about Football Information Bureau's relocation from Iowa to Ohio
	1972-04-25 Handwritten letter about the bureau
	1972-05-14 Hotel reservations in Birmingham
	1972-08-25 Letter about oddities in sports
	1972-10-10 About Southern Hospitality
	1972-12-24 FIB custodian – thanks for Christmas card
Vance, James E.	**1974-07-22** Senior Vice President First National Bank of Birmingham; congratulatory letter on up-coming honor in Knoxville on September 7, 1974
Wade, Wallace	**1935-02-09** Football Coach Duke University about Zipp's scoring system
Wagner, Frank A.	**1972-07-27** Director Birmingham Parks & Recreation, about Zipp's July 23 article
Wallace, Frank	**1971-04-30** Notre Dame University Memorial Library – asks for memorabilia
Wallace, Sam, Jr.	**1973-09-01** Sent Zipp copy of letter to Mr. Rutland about Birmingham plaza and exhibition hall
Willingham, Tom	**1970-02-25** 3-fold purpose (1) nominate (2) nominate (3) 1960s All-America
Winslett, Hoyt "Hu"	**1973-02-27** President of Dollarhide Camp, Inc. Thanks for Alabama Sports Hall of Fame
Winslett, Hoyt, Jr.	**1973-02-16** Gave Invocation at Alabama Sports Hall of Fame Induction Dinner; Associate Rector of Church of Nativity-Huntsville, son of Hoyt, Sr. "Hu"
Woodruff, George R.	**1972-07-31** University of Tennessee Athletics Director – Invitation to Honor Press, First Nighter
Woodward, A.H. "Rick"	**1934-01-29** Chair Woodward Iron Co. About his memoirs. Built Rickwood Field.
Word, Cecil B.	**1969-02-13** President W.J. Word Lumber Company, Scottsboro, Alabama. Congratulations on

Sources

Barber, Red. *Show Me the Way to Go Home*. Philadelphia, PA: Westminster Press, 1971.

Birmingham News Company. *Mirror of Our Times: More Than a Century*. Birmingham: Birmingham News, 1997.

Barra, Allen. *Rickwood Field: A Century in America's Oldest Ballpark*. New York: W.W. Norton & Company, ©2010.

Black, Art. *Showdown at Rickwood: Ray Caldwell, Dizzy Dean, and the Early Years of America's Oldest Ball Park, 1910-1931*. Birmingham, AL: Blue Rooster Press, 2017

Blackmon, Douglas A. *Slavery by Another Name: The Re-Enslavement of Black Americans from the Civil War to World War II*. New York: Anchor, 2009.

Burleson, Dick. *You Better Be Right! My 25 Years as an SEC Football Official*. [United States]: D. Burleson, ©2006.

Call, A. Jeffrey. *Rolling with the Tide*. Springville, UT: Bonneville Books, 2003.

Cook, Ben. *Good Wood: A Fan's History of Rickwood Field*. Birmingham, AL: R. Boozer Press, 2005.

Curtis, Brian. *Fields of Battle: Pearl Harbor, the Rose Bowl, and the Boys Who Went to War*. New York: Flatiron Books, 2016.

Dunnavant, Keith. *The Missing Ring: How Bear Bryant and the 1966 Alabama Crimson Tide Were Denied College Football's Most Elusive Prize*. New York City: Thomas Dunne Books, 2006.

Faber, Charles F., and Richard B. Faber. *Spitballers: The Last Legal Hurlers of the Wet One*. Jefferson, N.C.: McFarland & Company, Inc., Publishers, 2006.

Gaddy, Kenneth, ed. *Sixteen and Counting: The National Championships of Alabama Football*. Tuscaloosa: University Alabama Press, 2017.

Finebaum, Paul, and Gene Wojciechowski. *My Conference Can Beat Your Conference: Why the SEC Still Rules College Football*. New York, NY: Harper, 2014.

Glass, Eugene. *The Dog Fancier*. Battle Creek, MI: Eugene Glass, Volume 32, Number 11, 1923.

Glier, Ray. *How the SEC Became Goliath*. Nashville: Howard Books, 2012.

Hemphill, Paul. *Leaving Birmingham: Notes of a Native Son*. A Deep South Book. Tuscaloosa: University of Alabama Press, 2000.

The Heart of the Game: The Education of a Minor-League Ballplayer. New York: Simon & Schuster, 1996.

Liebendorfer, Don E. *The Color of Life is Red: A History of Stanford Athletics 1892 – 1972*. Palo Alto, California: Board of Trustees of the Leland Stanford Junior University, 1972.

McKiven, Henry M. Jr., *Iron and Steel: Class, Race, and Community in Birmingham, Alabama 1875-1920*. Chapel Hill: The University of North Carolina Press, 1995.

McWhorter, Diane. *Carry Me Home: Birmingham, Alabama*. Reissue ed. New York: Simon & Schuster, 2013.

Newman, Zipp. *The Impact of Southern Football*. Montgomery, Alabama: Morros Bell Publishing Company, 1969.

Pietrusza, David. *Judge and Jury: The Life and Times of Judge Kenesaw Mountain Landis*. South Bend, Ind.: Taylor Trade Publishing, 2001.

Railway Age, Volume 123, No. 10; September 6, 1947, "W.G. Peoples" history, page 78.

Rogers, William Warren; Robert David Ward; Leah Rawls Atkins; Wayne Flynt. Alabama: *The History of a Deep South State – Bicentennial Edition*. Tuscaloosa: The University of Alabama Press, 2018.

Scott, Richard. *SEC Football: 75 Years of Pride and Passion*. Minneapolis, MN: Voyageur Press, 2008.

Legends of Alabama Football. Champaign, IL: Sports Publishing, LLC., 2004.

Smith, Catherine Pittman. *Images of Mountain Brook*. Charleston, SC: Arcadia Publishing, 2014.

Stephenson, Creg and Kirk McNair. Always a Crimson Tide: .... Chicago: Triumph Books, 2011. 978-1600785948

Van Hoose, Alf. *More Than a Game: The Best of Alf Van Hoose*. Edited by Creg Stephenson. Fire Ant Books. Tuscaloosa: University of Alabama Press, 2009.

Wade, Don. *Always Alabama: A History of Crimson Tide Football*. New York: Touchstone, 2006.

Welden, Edgar, and Keith Dunnavant. *Time Out! A Sports Fan's Dream Year*. Birmingham, Ala.: Will Pub., 1999.

Whitman, Howard Jay. *A Brighter Later Life*. Upper Saddle River, NJ: Prentice-Hall, 1961.

Whitt, Timothy. *Bases Loaded with History: The Story of Rickwood Field, America's Oldest Baseball Park*. Birmingham, AL: R. Boozer Press, ©1995.

"Ol Zipp" *Newsweek*, Vol. XXXII No. 24, page 62, December 6, 1948.

Acknowledgements

Alabama Sports Hall of Fame and Museum
  Scott Myers, Executive Director

The Birmingham News-Age Herald microfilm archives at the Birmingham Public Library

Carolita Keith Cantrell (Dwight Keith Family Albums)

Morris Family Collection

Samford University Archives

Southern History Department of the Birmingham Public Library

* * *

Letters referenced and excerpted in this book are sourced from three collections:
(1) The Morris Family Collection
(2) The Birmingham Public Library Southern History Department – letters from 1920s through 1930s
(3) The Alabama Sports Hall of Fame & Museum – letters from 1940s through 1970s.

All picture images within this book are sourced from
The Morris Family Collection unless noted otherwise.

About the Author

Frances "Bee" Newman Morris is the daughter of "Zipp" Newman. She is married to Walter Morris, the mother of three children and grandmother of thirteen. She studied at Hollins College in Virginia and graduated from the University of North Carolina – Chapel Hill.

She is a member of the National Society of Colonial Dames of America in the Commonwealth of Virginia. She lives in Mountain Brook, Alabama.

+ + +

Worth Earlwood Norman, Jr., a native of Norfolk, Virginia, is a writer of biographies and history. He authored *James Solomon Russell*, published by McFarland & Company Publishers, and *William Jelks Cabaniss, Jr.*, published by Archdeacon Books. He has also authored two "Alabama Timeline" books: *Those Republicans* and *African American Entrepreneurs*.

A graduate of Old Dominion University, he is the father of three children and grandfather of six, and lives with his wife Patricia Ann Padrick Norman in Hoover, Alabama.

Seated: Walter F. Morris and Frances Newman Morris
Standing: Francie Morris Deaton, Walter F. Morris, Jr.,
Duncan T. Morris, Henry H. Morris

Bee & Walter Morris
with their grandchildren

162

Index

CPSIA information can be obtained
at www.ICGtesting.com
Printed in the USA
LVHW031149200519
618456LV00003B/348